Table Of Contents

Wicca For Beginners 2021:
Part 1,

An Introduction to Wiccan Beliefs

Wicca For Beginners 2021: Part 2,

An Introduction To Wiccan Magic and Rituals

Wicca For Beginners 2021: Part 1,

An Introduction to Wiccan Beliefs

Introduction

Congratulations on your purchase of the book *Wicca for Beginners*, and thank you for doing so.

This book will contain plenty of information on the history of Wicca and how it has evolved over the years. The following chapters will cover magic and spells with details on what they are and how to use them. You'll learn some starter spells in popular categories such as friendship, romance, and prosperity.

Not only will you learn about spells and how to cast them, but you'll also learn about the common tools used in Wicca and how they are used in spells and rituals.

After reading this book, you should have the information and knowledge you need to get started on your Wiccan path. You'll have a preliminary guide on the tools and equipment that you should procure to set up your altar and ritual space and have plenty of new spells to try out!

Hopefully, you will have fun getting your feet wet in this new Wiccan venture. This is a Beginner's Guide, and you are always encouraged to keep reading and expanding your studies. However, this is a great place to start! So, go ahead and turn to the next page.

Wicca is a popular topic, and there are so many books out there on the subject. Thank you for choosing to go with this one! Every effort was made to make sure this book is packed full of useful and fun information for you. We hope you enjoy it!

Chapter One: What Is Wicca?

It is time for you to take the first steps on your path as a newly practicing Wiccan. Here is your starting point. Whether you are ready to embrace the Wiccan lifestyle fully or you are interested in learning more about the craft before diving in, this is where you want to start!

You must have questions, like what is Wicca? What are the spells? What is magic? All of these questions will be answered. Take a look at the origins of Wicca to begin your journey.

Origins of Wicca

Wicca is best described as a modern-day religion that draws on the traditions of ancient witchcraft. While Witchcraft traditions still exist, they are different from Wicca. One can be a Wiccan without being a Witch. Contrary to what media and many other religions would have you believe, Wicca is not evil or destructive. Wicca is a harmonious religion that practices a peaceful and balanced way of life.

Although the ancient traditions have been obscured, rewritten, and removed from history, mainly during the medieval era, it is still possible to glean how those traditions were practiced and then modernize them. Through archeological discovery, the traditions of ancient witchcraft have been understood better.

A main concept of Wicca is pursuing and promoting oneness with the divine and everything that exists. Archaeologists and historians have found ample evidence to show that the original Witchcraft traditions worshipped a Fertility Goddess and a Hunter God. Cave painting evidence suggests that these traditions had been practice for at least 30,000 years. Many of the cave paintings also depict a group of people, such as a coven.

Wicca and Witch are words that derive from the Old English *Wicce*, which referred to a 'Wise Woman' or Healer. Essentially, the origin of Wiccans were women in a community who had knowledge of herbs and plants and used them as medicine and charms. A lot of these practitioners are also referred to as Shamans or Witch Doctors in other cultures.

Gerald Gardner and Doreen Valiente are often attributed with the founding of modern-day Wicca in the early to mid-1900s. Some of the inspiration came from familial traditions that were passed down from generations. Others came from known pre-Christian 'pagan' practices drawn from Ireland, Wales, and Scotland.

Gardner immersed himself in the British Occult during the 1950s and then began to develop a modernized belief system that centered on unity and worship of nature. Magic and spells, as well as the primary worship of a Fertility Goddess and worship of additional deities, such as the Horned God.

After developing his first Coven, Gardner, together with Valiente, worked with the other coven members to structure and write books on this new interpretation of Wicca.

By the 1960s, Wicca had spread to the United States. There was an emphasis on nature, unconventional lifestyles, and a pursuit for the divine and spirituality. Wiccan Covens began to form, usually with 11 to 15 members. Covens usually had a hierarchy of priests and priestesses and included their own structure. Covens encompassed the overall principles of Wicca but allowed the members to build their own traditions and gave them the freedom to include other aspects into their traditions.

Traditional Wicca or Gardnerian Wicca has branched out into many other traditions, such as Norse Wicca, Celtic Wicca, Druidism, Herbal Wicca, Faery Wicca, Eclectic Wicca, and Solitary Wicca.

A few of the common pillars of Wicca include the creed 'An' Harm None, do As you Will.' What this means is that if your actions do not intentionally or unintentionally harm someone else, you are free to do what you want. This includes daily activities, tasks, and even magic and spells!

Another important rule that falls into many of the Wiccan traditions is the Law of Three. This law dictates that whatever you put out into the universe is returned to you threefold. This includes positive and negative feelings, thoughts, and actions.

These two main principles outline how Wicca is more about personal growth, spirituality, striving for a better life, and making positive changes in the world.

While each tradition has its own practices and teachings, most traditions follow a typical or similar archetype that is the core of Wicca.

What Wicca Is

Wicca is both a lifestyle and a belief system. The Path of Wicca encourages practitioners to pursue spirituality, learn about the earth, and find a deeper understanding of the universe and deity. Wicca promotes free-thinking, individuality, and a deep connection to nature. The concept that every living thing is connected to the divine is prevalent in Wicca.

One of the most important lessons that Wicca teaches is responsibility. Wiccans accept responsibility for their actions as one of the important foundations of Wicca, rather than seeking an outside source or an entity of some kind as the cause of temptation or bad behavior. If a Wiccan messes up or does something that harms someone else, then the consequences fall on the Wiccan themselves, no one else.

More than that, Wicca is a celebration of the natural cycles of the planet—the seasons. It celebrates the lunar phases and implements the natural powers of nature, the world, and the universe to cast spells.

Wiccans work with their deities, not in servitude of them. They strive for a life of harmony, peace, and balance. Wiccan spells involve healing, prosperity, harmony, wisdom, creativity, friendship, and romance. Using the power of plants and trees, crystals and rocks, even animals, and the natural elements are how Wiccans harness magic, create spells, and direct their power.

The Goddess and God exist within everyone and everything. Wiccans believe that The Divine can be found in everything, from the smallest flower to the tallest tree. From the crawling ant to the largest whale. The Divine exists in rivers, ocean, clouds, rain, soil, and the air we breathe.

Magic is created from this divine energy. All creations come from combining the elements of earth, air, fire, and water. The sun, moon, and environment become teachers to Wiccans. Providing wisdom and knowledge that has been accumulated throughout the ages, accessing that magic is the source of Wiccan power. This belief creates profound and deep respect for the environment and nature, as well as all life forms.

Wiccans and witches have been persecuted for hundreds of years for their beliefs and practices. This history has created general secrecy regarding Wicca and its traditions. Secrecy isn't required unless it is a specific Coven rule. However, this violent history has also fostered a belief in religious freedom among the Wiccan community. The idea that Wiccan beliefs are not the only beliefs is powerful among Wiccans.

Religious freedom is a strong staple in Wiccan beliefs. Wicca is not the kind of religion that creates missionaries that travel to places to convert new members, growing their numbers and spreading their word. However, Wicca does not turn away those seeking knowledge and answers and those who have an interest in learning.

Overall, Wicca is balanced, peaceful, nature-oriented, and accepting. It is both a religion and a lifestyle that can be pursued by walking many paths, connecting one to the spirit and the divine that exist within everything on this earth.

What Wicca is can't be entirely summed up in a few words or even a few pages! Living the Wiccan lifestyle can be complicated, and it takes practice to understand and embrace the idea fully. It can be a hugely rewarding, empowering, and enlightening path to walk, however. Anyone who is interested is encouraged to learn what they can, find a teacher or a coven, and continue to take this amazing journey for themselves.

What Wicca Is Not

There are many stigmas surrounding Witchcraft and Wicca regarding what it is and what it isn't. Many of these negative stereotypes have been fueled by the media and entertainment industry. Horror movies and television shows with witches who worship the devil and cast hexes on their enemies have been circulating for years.

Prior to that, Witches and Wiccans were persecuted for their religious beliefs for centuries, primarily by the Catholic Church. Wiccans were said to worship Satan, sell their souls to the devil, and use the devil's power to cast magic and seduce people to their communities to follow Satan.

Unfortunately, there is one major flaw in this logic. The Devil or Satan is a Christian religious entity, not Wiccan.

For thousands of years before Catholicism and Christianity, Wiccans and Witches practiced their beliefs and provided their communities with healing and a connection to nature and the divine. They have never worshipped or believed in an evil entity, and that has been proven through the archeological study of cave paintings.

Now, since Wiccans don't believe in an entity such as the devil, how can they worship him? Well, the easy answer is they can't.

The Hunter God has often been depicted in cave paintings as a man wearing Stag antlers or as a man with a stag head. These portrayals of the Hunter God are a representation of his masculinity and his connection to the forest and the animals. Many ancient religious rituals and practices involve the wearing of animal skins or animal parts, such as feathers in Native American headdresses or furs that are worn by Shamans and Witch Doctors.

It could very well be a coincidence that Christianity developed an evil goat-like entity (similar to a stag) that symbolizes temptation, destruction, and evil. However, there is some evidence to suggest that such an entity was created in an attempt to convert people and communities away from Wicca and Witchcraft.

Please keep in mind that Wicca is not devil worship; it has never been about devil worship. If other religions have evil entities that are part of their theology, that isn't bad or wrong. Wicca, however, does not subscribe to such beliefs.

On a larger scale, Wiccans believe in doing the right thing because it is the right thing. They do not believe in an evil entity that threatens eternal damnation to keep them from behaving badly. Some people may need more structure and that firm guiding hand to remind them how they should live their lives.

Wicca is not a cult. Covens do not gather under a single, supreme leader that seeks to spread their word, recruit more members, and convert others to their faith. There is no extremism in Wicca, as Wicca is a very balanced, peaceful belief system.

Magic and spiritual power are drawn from the four elements, from nature, and from the universe. Wiccans do not steal power or the life force of other people or animals to cast their spells. Magic is a pure form of energy that is not manipulative or sourced by stealing life and strength from others.

On the subject of spells and magic, Wiccans do not use spells to cast hexes on others. They do not seek to control the hearts and minds of anyone else, and they do not destroy or disrupt the lives of others. Remember that first Law, 'An Harm None, Do as You Will?' That extends to spells and magic, too. That 'none' doesn't just apply to people, either. All life is included in that concept.

Of course, Wiccans aren't perfect. No one is, really. As humans, we can't always abstain from negative thoughts and feelings. Sometimes, we blame others and think we are the victims. The same flaws that exist in humans exist in Wiccans, as well.

While Wiccans believe that the Law of Three will correct any imbalances in thoughts and behavior, it is also important to make a conscious effort before performing a ritual or casting a spell. Sometimes, spells designed for the best intentions may end up having unwanted consequences. Wiccans try to carefully consider outcomes that could potentially affect others and how they will be affected.

There are many things Wicca isn't. If you have any concerns, keep reading, and decide for yourself. There are also communities you can join to get your questions answered if this book doesn't give you what you need. As always, you are encouraged to find answers and seek knowledge.

Altar and Tools

The Wiccan Altar is an important aspect of Wiccan practices. The altar is usually a stationary location that is used for casting spells, rituals, even meditations, and other Wiccan practices.

While your altar doesn't have to be stationary, many practitioners find it beneficial to have a designated location for practicing and casting magic. Magic and spells can be cast anywhere at any time. Many rituals are performed outside; some spells are cast in specific rooms of the house. A temporary altar can be set up for these occasions, or the ritual can be performed without an altar under these circumstances.

Every Wiccan's altar is going to be different. Some practitioners use a coffee table or bedside table with just a few candles. Others have a specially crafted table that has carved designs or a special tapestry on them. Some altars don't even have a table but are just a designated spot on the floor with a tapestry or blanket. When you begin to set up your own altar, do what feels right for you. The most decorative or expensive altar might look great, but if it doesn't flow with your energy or wishes in an altar, stick to what makes sense for you.

An altar can be as decorated or bare as you would like. There are some common tools that are often found on a Wiccan altar, though, and some are not such common tools.

Some basic altar designs or setups include having a candle at each of the four cardinal directions—north, east, south, and west—and objects to represent each of the four elements—earth, air, fire, and water. This includes a candle to represent both the Goddess and the God and objects to represent other deities, as well. Generally, there should be an incense burner since it is very commonly used in rituals and spells.

The more common tools usually found on a Wiccan's altar include the following:

- Athame
- Cauldron
- Chalice or goblet
- Mortar and pestle
- Wand
- Besom or Broom
- Grimoire or Book of Shadows

Now, if you decide to join a Coven, there is usually a central altar where your Coven gathers and a single Grimoire or Book of Shadows that the Coven defaults to. Every

Coven is going to be different. Whether or not individuals have their own altars or Grimoire is going to be specific to the Coven you joined.

Athame

An Athame is a black-handled, double-edged ritual knife. It is associated with the element of fire and masculine energy. Often, the Athame isn't even a sharpened blade, as it has more of a ritual symbolism than a tool used for cutting and slicing.

Athames are commonly used for carving symbols in candle wax, dirt, or sand. They can also be used to channel energy and lay down energetic barriers. Since the Athame is associated with fire, it can be set on your altar as the object that represents this element.

Cauldron

Cauldrons are commonly depicted in media and art as a large cast-iron pot over a fire with a boiling, goopy brew with several cloaked witches standing around it, mixing the potion. Cauldrons, however, have many, many uses.

Cauldrons come in many shapes and sizes. Some are only two inches across, while others can be thirteen inches across or large enough to cook an entire soup over an open fire. Some are bowl-shaped, and others are potbellied. Some cauldrons have lids and handles, while others don't. You might find a cauldron with feet while others sit on a flat bottom.

Most cauldrons are cast-iron or metal that is painted black. They can be used for many parts of a Wiccan ritual. Cauldrons make effective incense holders. They can also be a container for fire during fire rituals, as long as they are fire-safe metal or material. Cauldrons can be used to mix ingredients together, and if they are food-safe, they can be used to make brews, infusions, and other ingestible magical mixtures.

Whenever you mix ingredients that are meant to be consumed or used directly on the skin, make sure that the cauldron or other equipment that you are using has been labeled food-safe and heat-safe. Many cauldrons on the market today are painted black or not made of pure cast iron, and they can leak toxicity into the food being cooked.

Chalice/Goblet

A chalice or goblet is another versatile tool. They can be fancy and made of expensive metal and decorated with engravings and jewels, or it could be a simple carved wooden cup.

The chalice represents the element of water. It can be used in rituals for drinking libations and honoring the Goddess and God. Additionally, the chalice is associated with springtime but also the Magic Well. Many Celtic myths and legends include a reference to a Magic Well that can be the source of great power or used in divination (which will be covered more in a later chapter).

Mortar and Pestle

A mortar and pestle is a combination tool. It generally comes with a bowl-shaped base and a wide and broad grinding tool. The mortar and pestle can be placed on the altar or just easily accessible for spells and rituals.

A mortar and pestle are used to grind herbs, resins, seeds, and other plant materials that are used in magic. Whether it is to make a spell powder, your own incense, or a charm bag, a mortar and pestle are important in crafting herb magic.

Having a separate mortar and pestle strictly for food use and then one for ritual use is often recommended. There are many ways to incorporate magic in cooking and in the kitchen. If you have any interest in learning about food and cooking magic, having a mortar and pestle only for food is a good idea.

Wand

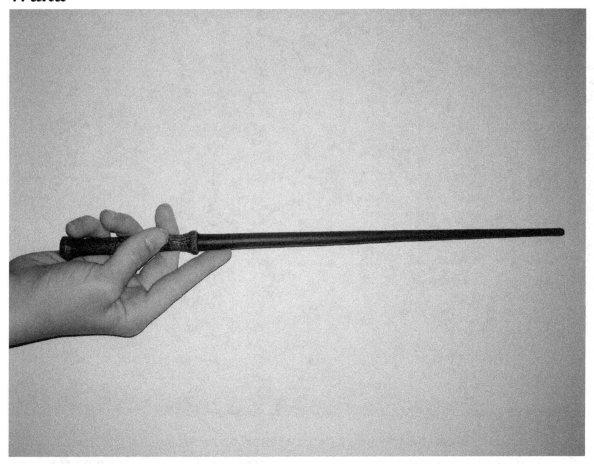

Wands are not an essential tool when it comes to Wicca. They also carry media stigmas, such as in the popular movie series *Harry Potter*, where wands are used by witches and wizards to cast spells.

A wand is a masculine object associated with the element air. Wands are versatile; they can be made of metal, wood, or any material, really. Some are hollow and filled with herbs and crystals; others might have runes carved on them or are more intricate and decorative.

Wands are used in channeling and directing magical power. They are not a key component in spellcasting or ritual. However, they can be instrumental when creating sigils for spells (sigils will be covered in greater detail in later chapters). When casting your Sacred Circle, the wand can help lay down a protective, energetic barrier.

Besom/Broom

Have you ever seen a movie with witches flying around on broomsticks? Or maybe you've seen a Halloween decoration of a witch on a broom in front of a full moon? Witches on brooms have served as popular decorations for Halloween and related holidays.

Did you know that brooms are actually used in Wicca? While you probably won't be taking any midnight flights on your own broomstick, brooms do have a symbolic meaning and use in ritual and Wicca.

The ritual broom is referred to as a Besom. They are commonly used in magic and spells meant for clearing away negative energies and cleansing a space or a room. The act of sweeping can be symbolic or real when using a Besom in ritual.

There are some beautifully crafted besoms on the market with feathers, ribbons, and fancy colors. However, like with all the ritual tools, choose the one that you resonate with most. Fancy and expensive brooms do not necessarily mean better. Magical tools are driven by their wielder's intention, not how they look or what they are decorated with.

Grimoire/Book of Shadows

Another term that has some media stereotypes is the Wiccan Book of Shadows. Covens usually keep a central Book of Shadows for all of their teachings. However, keeping your own isn't a bad idea. If you are a solitary practitioner, you definitely want to keep a Book of Shadows.

During the years of persecution, having a Book of Shadows could lead to a death sentence, which is why, sometimes, they were written in code. Some Covens still carry on that tradition, so the code may only be known to the High Priestess or High Priest of the Coven.

A Grimoire or Book of Shadows is a culmination of the information and knowledge you have gathered as a Wiccan. It also serves as a journal of your spiritual journey. These books tend to hold rituals, spells, and information on deities, histories of the Coven, or practitioner. You can also write down your thoughts, feelings, and experiences when performing rituals or spells in your Book of Shadows.

Some practitioners will write in their Book of Shadows every day. There is no right or wrong way to keep a Book of Shadows. If you are more artistically inclined, you might like to draw pictures and images to corresponding topics in your Book of Shadows. You may also like to print out pictures for the same effect. Or, you might only put written words in your Book of Shadows.

The book becomes a sacred text as you write it. Not only does it contain your spiritual and magical experiences, but it also contains your own practices and beliefs or your Coven's.

Many Wiccans like to make their own tools if they can. It can be very empowering, and they connect you with all the tools in your craft.

Ritual

While not all Wiccan traditions follow the same paths and principles, a common element in all traditions is a Ritual. Wiccan Ritual is at the core of many Wiccan practices. Whether it is to celebrate a lunar phase like New Moon or Full Moon, holidays such as the Esbats and Sabbats, or important milestones like handfasting (weddings), initiations, or life celebration ceremonies, a Ritual is performed in various forms for each.

If you belong to a Coven, then more often than not, your Coven will gather to perform such rituals together. However, if you are a solitary practitioner, performing rituals on your own is also important.

A ritual tends to be an event to honor the Goddess and God and celebrate the universe and how it works—the changing of the seasons or lunar phases, giving thanks for the harvest or making it through the winter.

Generally, no two Wiccan Rituals are the same. Covens tend to hold highly structured and elaborate rituals. On the flip side, sometimes, solitary practitioners will make up a ritual as they go along, rather than have a predetermined notion or choreography to follow.

The content of each ritual will vary based on what the ritual is for. A Full Moon ritual will be focused on The Goddess and honoring her. There are holiday celebrations that honor springtime and new beginnings or solstices. Some rituals will focus on the relationship between the Goddess and God and may venture into a more sexual nature.

While rituals vary from Coven to Coven, practitioner to practitioner, and tradition to tradition, there are some basic components to each ritual.

The elements of ritual include:

- Purification of participants and space
- Setting the Altar
- Casting the Sacred Circle
- Invocations
- Intention is Set
- Heart of Ritual is performed
- Thanking Deity
- Closing Sacred Circle

Purification for the practitioner or participants in the ritual can be in the form of a ritual bath or with smudging or another preferred method of purification. The space where the ritual is held should be purified as well.

Next, the altar should be set, often at the center of where the sacred circle is being cast. Casting the circle can be a type of ritual in itself, especially in a Coven, and it creates a barrier between the practitioners and the rest of the world. During the invocations, this is generally when the Goddess and God are invited to join the ritual, as well as the elements earth, air, fire, and water.

Once invocations are complete, an intention for the ritual should be set. This intention should be in line with the goal of the ritual. If it is an initiation ritual, the intention could be that all new initiates are fully welcomed into the circle. If it is a harvest ritual, the intention could be as simple as to give thanks for the bountiful harvest.

The heart of the ritual is where many different tasks can be performed for honoring. Sometimes, covens will put on a dramatic scene. A solitary practitioner might write a poem and read it aloud. There can be a time for spellcasting, meditation, divination, and other magical practices that enhance rituals, as well. Many rituals include dancing, chanting, or drumming of some kind.

Many rituals will designate a time for cakes and wine, which is a kind of ritual feasting where portions of the food and drink are offered to the Goddess and God.

Once the tasks of the ritual are complete, it is always important to thank your deities and properly close your sacred circle. You may find that you need to ground yourself after a ritual. This is common.

Rituals are quite subjective, and as you practice, you will get a feel for performing tasks that are oriented toward your ritual's intention. Stick to what feels right for you, and you'll begin to develop your own methods for rituals.

Chapter Two: What Is Magic?

The word magic has had many meanings and uses throughout history. Commonly, magic refers to using tricks and illusions to portray magical events. Performers have used these illusions for hundreds of years as a form of entertainment.

Some popular illusions include pulling a rabbit out of a hat and escape artists freeing themselves from potentially deadly and impossible situations. Magic with clown cars, where a bunch of clowns emerges from a tiny car, is a type of illusion magic, as well as the magic where the person who manages to get your watch off your wrist while talking to you, without you noticing!

This kind of magic is purely for entertainment value.

For Wiccans, magic isn't an entertainment platform. Magic is a skill and tool that is used as part of the Wiccan lifestyle. In terms of Wicca and Witchcraft, the word magic is defined as the art of intentionally directing the co-creative forces of the universe by directing natural and universal energy to effect desired changes.

Everything is made up of energy. Modern-day science has the equipment to measure energy in the form of heatwaves, sound waves, light waves, and several other forms. These types of equipment can measure the energy fields in and around any kind of object. Electrical currents exist within all living creatures, including humans. The earth itself has a molten lava core that is composed of heat and light energy.

Wiccans have spent thousands of years studying these energies, learning about how each type of energy has power and how it can be used to make changes. A change can be as small as healing a headache or having softer skin, or as complex as calling a rainstorm or another weather change.

Energies interact with each other naturally. Wiccans can influence and direct those natural energies to interact differently. This is what creates magic.

Generally speaking, Wiccans use magic to improve their lives and circumstances. Magic is frequently used to improve health, prosperity, love, protection, and overall well-being. That doesn't mean that magic can't be used for someone else. It is imperative, however, to get permission from someone else if you plan to cast a spell or use magic on their behalf.

The rule 'An Harm None, Do as You Will' is very important when it comes to magic. Magic can be used with the best of intentions, but if you cast a spell for someone without their permission, you could be forcing them to deal with something they aren't ready to face or pushing them out of their comfort zone without their consent. This is frowned upon.

Additionally, using magic to get your way with someone, such as a love spell cast on a specific person, is again forcing your will on someone else, and that is not appropriate. Magic isn't meant to control someone else, hurt other people, or disrupt the balance of their lives. You'll just need their expressed permission if you want to use magic for their sake.

Intention and magical goals are two important components when making magic. Regardless of your method or tradition, intention and goal are both keys to making successful magic. Before you begin casting magic, set your intention, and know your goal. This will help ensure success.

Magic today is varied. Depending on the tradition you follow, you may only learn about certain types of magic. You may only have a personal interest in one type and never expand beyond that. Most Wiccans lean toward natural elements and tools when creating magic. Sometimes, no tools are needed at all, such as when you decide to create magic through dancing and chanting.

Types of Magic:

- Candle Magic
- Cord Magic
- Charms and Sachets
- Talismans and Amulets
- Herb Magic
- Divination
- Manifestation
- Dancing/Movement and Chanting/singing
- Sigils

You'll discover your preferred forms of magic. You may want to dabble in a few different types to get a better understanding of magic as a whole. Don't be afraid to keep studying and learning more about magic and the various ways to use magic!

Most of the more commonly used magical methods are based on some folklore or older traditions from Celtic Lore and other ancient civilizations. These were some of the first practices of Wiccans from early civilizations. However, some methods are drawn from older Occult sources, specifically more ceremonial magic.

Candle Magic

Candle magic is pretty self-explanatory. Magic can be created through the burning of a candle. If you set your intention and goal and burn a candle while focusing on and visualizing that intention and goal, that intention is released into the universe as the candle burns.

Candle magic can be enhanced by anointing the candle with essential or herbal oils. You can carve runes or symbols into the candle wax to increase the potency of the magic. Also, selecting a candle that has a color appropriate to your intention and goal is another way to enhance the magic in candles.

Candle magic can be very basic and only include one candle. Sometimes, when casting specific spells with candles, you might need more than one, and a spell can sometimes call for candles of a specific color.

Not all magic has to be ceremonial and ritualistic. Candle magic is a great example of how simple some magic can be! The simplicity of a spell doesn't reduce its effectiveness, however.

Before using a candle in a spell, it is a good idea to cleanse the candle. You can do this by passing it through the smoke of burning incense or submerging it in a dish of sea salt.

Usually, when using candle magic, you'll want to burn the candle for three consecutive nights while it is sitting on your altar. You can repeat your intention or goal while it burns or visualize your goal. Including chanting and music is another great way to add magical potency to your spell.

Once the three nights are complete, keep the remaining candle stub in a magical place, or bury it in the ground.

Knot Magic

Knot magic is a form of magic that is primarily designed to store magical power and intention and then release it over a period of time.

To start, you'll want a 9-inch piece of string or cord. You can use a 9-foot cord, as well, if you are not planning on storing your cord in a small space. You can keep magic stored in the knots for as long as you need and then release them at a more appropriate time.

For a typical knot magic spell, you are going to be tying 9 knots. Start on the left end, then the right end. The third knot will be tied in the middle of the cord. You'll then keep tying the new knot between the two most recently tied while alternating from the left side to the right side.

As you tie each knot, visualize your goal and say the following chant for each knot.

By knot 1, the spell has begun
By knot 2, it cometh true
By knot 3, so mote it be
By knot 4, magic power I store
By knot 5, this spell's alive
By knot 6, this spell I fix
By knot 7, my goal I'll leaven
By knot 8, this will be fate
By knot 9, what's done is mine

Once each knot has been tied, your power is stored. The knots should be tied in one ritual, but they can only be released one knot a day once you start. They should be released in the same order in which they are tied. Untie your knots over nine consecutive days to release the stored magic into the universe toward your goals.

Before untying a knot, hold the cord in your hand and re-visualize your goal. Speak it aloud if that will help, and untie the knot to release the magic.

Knots don't just have to be used in this standard knot ritual. Magical knots are also used in handfasting ceremonies and joining spells and magic. Knots can hold power, combine energies, and bind energies together.

Charms and Sachets

Charms and sachets can essentially be the same thing. Generally, a charm or sachet is a bag of cloth or a pouch that has been filled with herbs or other magical catalysts, such as crystals or personal power items. These bags or pouches can be carried on a person or placed in a specific area for the magic to spread.

Some Wiccans will purchase premade pouches, while others prefer to make their own out of cloth and string. The color of the pouch can improve the spell potency, as can the type and color of yarn or string used to bind the sachet.

When making a sachet or charm bag, you'll want to lay the pouch and add your magical ingredients to the pouch. Sometimes, there is an incantation to go along with the assembly of your charm bag. Other times, there is an order in which your ingredients should be added. While making your charm bag, visualization of your intention is important.

You should assemble your charm or sachet on your altar.

Sachets can be carried on your person, in a pocket, purse, or backpack. They can be placed under your pillow, hung in a closet, or set in the glove compartment of your car. Generally, the spell you cast will give specifics about where your sachet should be placed.

Additionally, you should give your charm bag a squeeze periodically to release the magical power. When you do this, remember to visualize your goal and intention. This will continue to enhance the magical power.

Talismans and Amulets

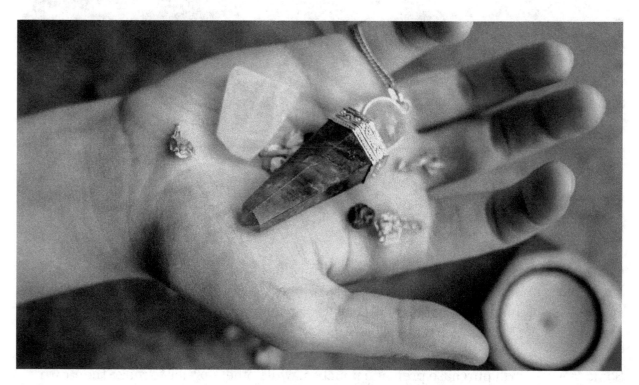

Talismans are manmade objects that are imbued with magical powers. Amulets are natural objects charged with magic and enhanced by their existing natural magical power.

A talisman can be a ring, a pendant, a coin, a figurine, or any object that is manmade, usually small enough to wear or keep in a pocket or bag.

Amulets can be crystals, rocks, a piece of bark, a feather, and objects existing in nature. Since these objects are already connected to their own source of natural magic, sometimes choosing an amulet with associations that align with your intention and goal is a great idea when making magic!

Before charging a talisman or amulet, you'll want to cleanse it by passing it through incense smoke, submerging it in sea salt, or using another preferred cleansing method.

Talismans and amulets are both used to enhance personal power. To charge them with magic, you'll want to set the object on your altar or hold it in your hand while sitting at your altar. Using clear visualization, create your magical intention and goal.

You can anoint talismans and amulets with essential or herbal oils to increase magical potency. You can sing or chant or play music over them or while holding them to increase the magical power.

Once fully charged, you'll want to keep your talisman or amulet on your person for three days, then keep it in a magical place. While wearing it, periodically touch your talisman or amulet, and when you do, clearly visualize your magical goal.

Charged objects are incredibly powerful. Once charged, that object is going to be aligned with a specific goal or intention. When you carry it on you, that charged energy will mix with your own energy to enforce the desired outcome.

You may have seen some jewelers selling charged pendants or rings. Any charged object can be powerful. However, talismans and amulets that you charge yourself are going to work the best for your own goals and desires.

Herb Magic

Herbal magic is again pretty self-explanatory. Magic and spells that are cast with the use of fresh plants, flowers, or plant parts, as well as dried herbs, flowers, and plant parts. Even herbal oils and essential oils qualify as herb magic.

Herb magic has a wide variety of uses. Making and burning herbal incense is a form of herb magic. Cooking with magical herbs makes a meal magical. Soaking in an herb bath adds magic to regular bathing.

Plants, flowers, trees, and herbs all contain powerful magic. They grow out of the earth and receive nutrients from the sun and water, and they breathe our air. Plants are a great combination of the four natural elements and their associated powers.

Most herbs have both medicinal and magical properties. Learning to utilize both magic and medicine is a great use of a Wiccan's power and talent. Natural medicine is incredibly potent and has significantly fewer side effects than more conventional medicines.

Some common types of herb magic include:

- Incense burning
- Herbal charm bags
- Magical cooking
- Herbal baths
- Herbals teas
- Herbal body products and cosmetics

If you use soap, lotion, shampoo, perfume, or other hygiene and cosmetic items, making your own with essential oils or dried herbs is a great way to benefit from herbal magic. Any time you craft something with herbs, you'll want to visualize the desired goal while making that item. When soaking in an herb bath, visualization of your intention is key, as well as when you cook an herbal meal, burn incense, and drink herbal tea.

The magical and medicinal properties of the individual herbs greatly enhance spells and magic. However, intent and desire are still important to the direction and creation of magic.

Herbs can easily be combined to make powders and placed in sachets and charms. An herbal powder constructed from the right herbs can be sprinkled in doorways for protection of the home.

Burning incense in a new home or smudging with an herb bundle can cast out negative or unwanted energies.

Natural ingredients, such as plants and herbs, are so potent in magical power. You can grow and harvest your own herbs, as many Wiccans geared toward herbal magic like doing. Most herbs and plant pieces can be harvested without killing the plant as well.

If you do harvest your own herbs and plants, it is important to remember to ask permission from the plant, give thanks, and also leave a gift to the plant and Earth Goddess. This goes any time you take something out of nature, including amulets. When you take something, you always have to give something back. This is a balance, and this is how you show your appreciation to the deity.

Divination

If you've ever seen a movie with a Gypsy, Shaman, or Witch casting runes, bones, or using tarot cards, then you've seen some commercial interpretations of divination.

Divination is a type of magic in which the Wiccan practitioner is seeking answers or direction. They use a catalyst to raise magical energy in order to receive guidance. Divination does require the practitioner to enter a light meditative state and to focus and visualize their question or concern strongly.

Divination isn't just about finding answers, though. Sometimes, it is about finding clarity or discerning the proper path or direction or action to take.

Common forms of divination include:

- Tarot Cards
- Runes
- Scrying (crystal ball, a bowl of water, black mirror, fire)
- Ouija Board/Witch Board
- Dousing (pendulum, dousing or divining rods)

There are many different kinds of tarot cards. Some are more traditional with the major and minor arcana, and others are more specialized to angels or Shamans. There are many ways to use Tarot cards for divining. You can do complex card spreads for yourself or just draw a single card every day. Many Wiccans who practice Tarot will draw a card every morning to help set the tone of their day.

Rune sets are usually based on the Nordic Runes of the Vikings. Like Tarot cards, runes can be spread in a specific layout for guidance. They can also be cast or scattered out on your altar for a more randomized spread.

Scrying is a form of divination where the practitioner enters a light meditative state and stares into a catalyst, such as a crystal ball, and receives information, often in the form of images that can then be interpreted as answers.

The Ouija Board or Witch Board is most commonly seen as a children's board game now, but that doesn't mean there isn't power in it. Ouija boards can communicate with many different entities, including spirits, angels, and darker entities. Without the proper intention and protections set, they can potentially let negative energies and entities into your space. However, if used correctly, there is a lot to be learned from the spirits that can be contacted.

Dousing is the process of using a pendulum or dowsing rods to follow energetic currents. If you ask a pendulum a question, it'll swing in one direction for 'yes' and another direction for 'no.' Several Wiccans carry pendulums with them and pull the pendulum out of their pocket or purse to answer daily questions for themselves.

Whenever you use divination, there should be an overall intention or goal to receive the information that serves your highest good. Some forms of divination require more in-depth study or practice with meditation to master.

In most cases, the information you receive from divination will need to be translated. If you ever do divination reading for yourself, write down everything you see, feel, learn, or read. At first glance, it might not make sense. Then think about your question or goal and play around with what you have written until it starts to makes sense.

When pursuing divination, it is important to remember that nothing is set. Any action, no matter how small, can alter the course that you are on. If you use divination to answer a question for yourself, the answer you receive is only relevant if you stay on the exact path you are on at the time you ask the question.

That said, how can you ever really learn anything from divination? Well, first of all, more than one road leads to the same destination. What that means is that multiple choices might bring you to the same resolution. There isn't ever a single right or wrong way to get to where you want to be or where you are meant to be.

Using divination magic is more of a way to guide yourself or even find out what you need to do to get to where you want to be. Life is always changing.

Manifestation

The art of manifestation is often something we do every day without even realizing it. However, when combined with magical power, manifestation can become much more potent and effective.

Manifestation is the act of desiring something and willing it into being. For example, if you want to buy a house and you spend a few minutes every day focusing your energy on manifesting the perfect house for your needs and wants, you'll be surprised at how fast you'll come across your heart's desire.

A few keys to proper manifestation include visualizing your goals as if they have already happened. Thinking in terms of 'I am' or 'I have,' rather than 'I want' or 'I will.' Align yourself with wish fulfillment, release your unlimited consciousness, and acknowledge and accept your strong personal power and connection to the divine.

A great time to incorporate manifestation into daily practices is during meditations. Speaking manifestations aloud enforces their power and strength. Phrase them in a way that sounds like it has already come to pass. Write it one on a piece of paper every day and then burn that paper every night to release the magical intention to the universe.

A manifestation is a powerful tool for getting what you want. It isn't an instant process, however. Sometimes, the intent has to be put out into the universe multiple times or repeatedly before the energies start to work for you. Clear and strong visualization is going to make manifesting more powerful.

Dancing/Movement and Chanting/Singing

As previously touched on, energy exists in heatwaves and sound waves. That energy becomes magic! Moving the body through dance creates heat, and singing, chanting, or even playing a drum or rattle creates sound waves. These are both forms of raising magical power that have been used for thousands of years.

Ancient rituals include drum circles, dancing around bonfires, and chanting invocations and incantations to the Goddess and God. Dancing and music are some of the oldest forms of magical power in human society.

Even before there was human speech or the concept of dance, movement could be used. The ritual of hunting or running through the woods to spear a prey is a very old form of magical power and expression that has been used since the early man. Different instruments like drums, rattles, and dried gourds have been incorporated in ritual and magic for a very long time as well.

Our bodies are full of magical power. Movement and voice belong to us personally and can create an empowered feeling when working magic. Additionally, our own bodies and voices add a touch of personal power to spells and magic that only enhance their effectiveness.

During a spell or ritual, adding a chant or incantation can increase the chances of success of that spell. Dancing around your circle during a spell will also continue to raise that energy and your success. When dancing or chanting, remember to keep visualizing your intention for the magic.

Sigils

Sigils are a unique form of magic in a way that you can never use the same one twice. There are many methods for drawing and creating your own sigils, but the basic idea is to visualize a goal in the form of a sentence or phrase.

Write that sentence or phrase down on paper. First, cross out any repeating letters. Some Wiccans will take out any vowels, as well. However, you can choose whether you want to leave the vowels or not. Next, you are going to break the remaining letters down to their most basic geometrical shapes.

For example, an H will be broken down into | - | and an O would become ( ). Once you've done this with all the letters, you can combine and rearrange the basic shapes into a pleasing arrangement for yourself.

After you have your sigil as you want it, surround it with a circle, square, or triangle shape.

While creating your sigil, you will want to read your intention aloud and continue to visualize it.

Once the sigil is created, you can use a finger or your wand to draw the sigil on yourself, on objects, and on walls, and continue to visualize. When you draw the sigil, the magical intention is released into whatever it is drawn on.

You can further activate sigils with meditation, crystals, or charging it with personal power.

Once the sigil has been used, dispose of your paper copy. Many Wiccans will burn their sigils once they have been cast. While disposing of them isn't necessary, sigils are designed for single use. They are not designed to linger. Rather, they become part of the universe and work their magical purpose subtly. Once released, their magic is constant.

There are many different ways to make your own sigils, and there is no right or wrong way to create or activate them. Play around with it, and see what works for you.

Magic comes in many forms and has many uses. It can be called forth and directed in so many different ways. You don't always need special tools and ingredients when making magic. Magic can be simple and complex. Different kinds of magic can be combined for more complex spells and increase magical potency.

Please remember that when making magic, even with strong visualization and intention, the magic needs reinforcement from you to keep working. Consider this; if you cast a spell to get a job, but you never search for or apply for any jobs, more than likely, the magical energy will fizzle out.

If you do not continue to reinforce your intention and goal, then your magic may never reach its destination, and the spell becomes unsuccessful. Magic is powerful, and so are you!

Chapter Three: What Are Spells?

We've talked about what magic is, as well as the different kinds of magic. So then, what is a spell? How does it differ from magic? How do you cast a spell?

These are very good questions!

Spells do not constitute waving a magic wand or saying magical words and having all your wishes and desires granted immediately. Movies and television shows seem to think that is how magic works. The magic that is locked away in every being and object on the planet is much more subtle but still powerful!

Magic is a broader term to describe the energy and the power Wiccans have to direct and change the course of that energy to achieve their goals.

Spells are the catalyst by which Wiccans use magic for their goals and intentions.

Essentially, casting a spell is a Wiccan's ability to perform a magical task that affects energetic change.

Spells are small rituals in a sense. They can be as simple as the burning of a single candle or the singing of a song. They can be more complex with various ingredients, tasks, and incantations.

Spells have been used since Ancient Egyptian society, as well as ancient Greek, Roman, and Nordic societies. These are some of the earliest known civilizations that used sigils, sacred circles, wands, and magical words.

A few common components of spellcasting include visualizing and stating your intention and goal. It also includes raising magical power in yourself and around you and then releasing that power out toward your desires. Once the spell is cast, reinforcing the magic over the next few days will ensure a greater chance of success with spells.

A basic spell commonly involves an incantation, the implementation of tools or ingredients, and a set of actions. Together, these components direct the spell's intention and energy to effect change properly.

While there isn't necessarily a right or wrong way to perform spells, it is a good idea to have a plan in mind or a written spell to cast before you start. Trying to make them up as you go isn't wrong, but as a beginner, it is a good idea to get used to spellcasting first. Sometimes spells are organized and call for a specific order of events or ingredients.

The magic of spells can also be influenced by outside forces, such as the lunar cycles and seasons. While there are recommended times to cast certain spells, this is not a requirement. If someone needs a healing spell or requests a healing spell, it would be inappropriate to tell them you had to wait three weeks for the moon to be in the proper cycle. The individual might not have that time or want to wait.

That said, let us take a look at lunar cycles and how they can impact spells.

During the waxing moon, when the moon is growing to its full state, it is an ideal time to cast spells for new beginnings, growth, initiations, enhancements, inspiration, freedom, vitality, love, prosperity, friendship, health, and luck. Generally, spells that draw something to you are best cast during the waxing moon.

On the night of the full moon, the best spells to cast include spells for manifesting goals, passion, healing, strength, knowledge, power, love, dreams, legal matters, protection, divination, and finding new employment. Any kind of spell that is strongly goal-oriented or seeking fruition of manifestations can be cast on the full moon.

When the moon is waning, going from the full state to the new state, it is a great time to cast spells to banish evil, remove obstacles, neutralize enemies, remove harm, banish illness, and banish addiction. This is the time to cast spells that banish, remove, or end any unwanted action, behavior, or energy.

At the New Moon, it is a good time to cast spells for new beginnings, new ventures, love, romance, good health, and job hunting. It's a good time to cast spells that involve anything new.

When considering the seasons, springtime is the season for casting spells that have to do with new beginnings, growth, starting over and overcoming hardships. It's a good time to cast spells for fertility, love, and cleaning out the old.

Summer is a great time to cast spells for weddings or marriage. This is also the time for magic focused on male fertility and energy, as well as legal contracts.

During the fall, spells to harvests, endings, and legal contracts are at their strongest.

Winter is the time to cast spells for family connections, hearth and home, and new beginnings. This is also the time of the Sun God returning from the underworld.

Spells are not designed to be used to manipulate, control, or dominate anyone else. These magics are essentially forbidden and are strongly frowned upon. It goes back to that original law we discussed of 'An Harm None, Do as You Will.' That law is going to continue to surface in your Wiccan studies.

For example, and this is a common one, you have a crush on someone, or you are in love with them, and you want them to love you back. It is commonly thought that casting a love spell directly on someone is the best way to gain their affections. Unfortunately, that isn't the case. Casting a spell that directs someone else's affections to be altered or changed is considered harmful and manipulative.

Here's a scenario. What if you cast that love spell on a specific person, but you realize they smell bad, or you find that you don't really like them, or they become obsessive? Even worse, what if they turn out to be abusive or manipulative or constantly unfaithful? Now you have altered someone's feelings for your own gain, and you won't even want to be in a relationship with them.

This is a very good example of why you should not cast a spell directly on someone else.

An alternative spell to cast is a 'bring love to me' spell (which will be covered in greater detail in the Romance Spells chapter). These spells don't target a specific person but open you up to attracting someone that is good for you and vice versa.

Spells should be geared toward improvement, balance, harmony, peace, and personal growth. Even so, the Law of Three states that any energy someone puts out into the world, positive or negative, will come back threefold. For Wiccans who don't follow the Harm None law, they will receive their own form of energetic backlash.

Generally, when following the Wiccan lifestyle, casting spells for positive change and resolution are more appealing to a Wiccan than anything negative.

So, what are spells? Spells are the ritual that Wiccans use to invoke and direct magical energies and power to create positive changes. Spells should always be cast with the intention of serving the highest of all involved.

While Wiccans primarily cast spells for their own desires and intentions, you can cast spells for others. It is important to have the expressed permission of someone else before casting a spell on their behalf. This is to continue to uphold the Harm None law. Even if you cast spells with the best of intentions, but without permission, you are imposing a change on a person without their consent. This can unintentionally cause harm.

Don't be afraid of spells and magic, though. Once you learn to cast spells and access that magic, you may learn more about yourself and your path than you ever thought possible!

Spells are pretty great and can be used for just about anything, as long as no one is being harmed. As you read through the types of spells, you may notice that they pertain to a lot of tasks, actions, and desires. Sometimes, they are so mundane you might be asking yourself, "Is magic even necessary for that?"

The truth is, casting a spell isn't always necessary. However, Wiccans often find empowerment in casting spells. It gives them a deeper sense of control over their own life and fate. It creates a sense of positivity around certain feelings and situations. Spells do not only affect change in the world, but the practitioner also feels the change within themselves.

When your own energy changes, the world you live in begins to change as well.

So what do spells do for you? First of all, spells align your energetic vibration with your personal goals and desires. Second, spells put your intentions and desires out into the universe, allowing the universe to help guide you. Third, spells allow you to let go so that your conscious mind doesn't interfere with how your intentions are manifested.

How to Cast Spells

The actual act of casting a spell does generally require some ceremony. Not all spells have to be cast at your altar; however, this is going to be the main base for your casting.

Before you even start your spell, make sure you have all your needed supplies and ingredients at your altar. Once you start casting, you don't want to have to run off and grab something you forgot! Also, keep your Book of Shadows close and your spellbook, if you are using one.

You'll want the four elements represented on your altar. Fire can be a lit candle; air can be burning incense. Water can be as simple as a glass of water, and the earth could be a rock or pebble. If you have a fixed altar, you can get more creative as desired with the representations on your altar.

For spellcasting, you will also want candles and some kind of physical representation of the Goddess and God or whatever deities you appeal to.

Before getting into the spellcasting, you are going to want to cast your Sacred Circle. This circle will serve as a barrier between you and outside energies. It will prevent any energies from encroaching on your spell that does not serve its purpose.

There are many ways to cast a Sacred Circle, and some are very simple, while others are more complex.

A basic circle casting involves setting your altar at the center of your intended circle, then placing your rock or pebble at the north corner, your glass of water at the west corner, your lit candle at the south corner, and the burning incense at the east corner.

Holding your wand, start facing east and invoke air while standing in the east. Then walk in a deosil (clockwise) circle to the candle to invoke fire, then water in the west, and the earth in the north. Complete your circle back in the east.

Alternatively, you can stand at the center of your circle and face each direction, starting in the east and turning deosil (clockwise).

Basic elemental invocations can sound like:

> *Here do I call in Air at the East, to fill my circle with the breath of life*
>
> *Here do I call in Fire at the South, to fill my circle with warmth and strength*
>
> *Here do I call in Water at the West, to cleanse my circle and fill it with life*
>
> *Here do I call in Earth at the North, to create a strong foundation for my circle*

Step to the center of your circle and stand at your altar to invoke the deity. You can continue to hold your wand or set it down.

An invocation for deity could sound like:

> *Mother Goddess and Father God, I invite that you join my circle, that you guard and guide me during this spell*

Once the invocations are made, you can complete the circle by saying:

> *I create sacred space, so mote it be*

Now that your circle has been cast, it is time to start preparing your spell. Sit in front of your altar and first close your eyes and take a few long, deep breaths. At this point, you should state your intention and visualize the goal of your spell.

Once you have a clear picture in your mind, begin to move through the designated tasks and actions of your spell. Keep your visualization strong during these actions and tasks to enhance the spell's power further.

The next step is to raise magical power and energy for your spell. This can be done through focused imagination and visualization. Really see your goal coming true and envision it as if the spell has already worked its magic.

Other methods of raising power include:

- Dancing
- Chanting
- Singing
- Incantation
- Playing an instrument (drum, rattle, flute, recorder, etc.)

As you raise the power, feel the magic stirring within you and around you. The power comes from within, but it also comes from the world and the universe. As power is raised, you'll be able to feel it. Sometimes, it takes practice and time for you to feel magic, but keep yourself open to magic and power.

After you have raised and focused your power, you may find yourself needing to ground yourself again. That energy can fill you up and make you feel a little dizzy or light-headed.

To ground yourself, sit cross-legged, and put your hands on the floor or ground. If you are outside, touch a rock or a tree. If you have crystals, rock salt, or tree bark inside, hold or touch something earthy to help yourself connect back to your body.

Once you have released your power, your spell will begin to work. You can continue to stay in your circle and meditate or close your Sacred Circle.

When closing your circle, thank the deity and elements. You can thank them individually or all at once. An example of a thanking incantation can sound like:

Thank you, Goddess, God, and the four elements for joining in my Circle. This circle is undone but not broken. Merry did we come here, merry do we part, to merry come again.

You'll want to extinguish your candles and clean up your space after.

When casting spells, if you make a charm or use an amulet or talisman, most spells will indicate whether you are supposed to bury the object, carry it on your person for any amount of time, keep it under your pillow, or hang in a specific space.

Since the magic continues to work after the spell is cast, it is important to follow these instructions to enhance the success of the spell.

Additionally, continue to visualize and take steps to accomplish your goals. Your spell will need continued participation from you to keep the magic working.

Spellcasting isn't limited to just your altar or sacred space that you have designated for practicing Wicca. Spells can be cast pretty much anywhere, as long as you have the tools and supplies you want or need for a given spell.

If you are casting a spell in a location other than at your altar, you should still be invoking a deity, the four directions, and setting an intention for a safe space. While you don't necessarily need a full Sacred Circle, holding a safe and protected space for yourself will prevent outside energies from influencing your spell.

A simple space holding intention can sound like:

I intend that this (room, car, space, etc.) becomes a safe and sacred space for my spellcasting.

Types of spells that may need to be cast in a designated location away from your altar include:

- Room cleansing
- Home protection
- Weather dances
- Fire rituals (should be performed around a safe fireplace or woodstove if inside or around a closed fire pit outside. Always adhere to local fire laws and safety.)
- Car protection

Depending on the kinds of spells that you find yourself casting, having a mini or portable altar is another option if you do not want a fixed location for your altar. Some Wiccans will keep an altar inside their house and a separate altar outside their house for outdoor rituals and spells.

Spellcasting can be creative and subjective. When you first start, you will probably be looking for prewritten spells to try. This book has plenty of those! However, you may find that you want to start writing your own spells, too.

Spellcrafting

Spellcrafting is the art of writing and designing your own spells. While it is recommended that you start out with prewritten spells, many Wiccans enjoy making their own.

Why write your own spells if so many are readily available? Sometimes Wiccans write spells out of necessity if they haven't found the specific kind of spell they want to cast. Sometimes, Wiccans will write spells or adapt spells based on what ingredients and tools are available to them. Then some Wiccans just prefer to create their own spells for a personal flare, just as they prefer making their own tools for the craft.

Adding your own personal power to spells by writing them is going to help them align with your energy. Spells aligned with your personal energy are more effective for your goals.

Writing spells is a little bit of a learned skill. This is primarily because of all the different variable sin spells. Magic comes from so many forms, candles, colors, herbs, chanting, crystals, etc. Understanding the magical and medicinal properties of the ingredients that go into spells is going to be necessary for writing your own spells.

For example, if you are writing a spell for love, you'll want to include ingredients and tools that resonate with the feeling of love, such as a Rose Quartz, or pink flower petals, or a red candle.

Having a basic knowledge and understanding of common spell ingredients is recommended if you are interested in writing your own spells.

The good news is that spells don't have to be masterfully written or composed as poetry. Many incantations rhyme or have a flowing pattern to them, but that isn't necessary. Generally, spells written as couplets or in rhyme tend to be easier to remember. If you are writing your spells down, then you can always refer back to them.

To write a spell, you will first need to know your intention or goal. It is a good idea to start with a piece of paper and write your intention, then let the ingredients, incantation, and spell actions unfold. Once you have everything together, you can write it out as formally or informally as you'd like in your Book of Shadows.

Let's say you want to attract money. At the top of your paper, write 'Attract Money.'

Next, list some colors and ingredients that go along with money and wealth. Write them down, in this case, 'Green, patchouli, basil, and sage.'

This is going to be a very simple money spell, so the two spell ingredients are going to be a green candle and patchouli essential oil.

Now we should write our incantation. You might need to throw some words down and see what starts to sound right or what resonates with you. This specific money incantation will look like:

> *Bring more money to me*
> *This is my will, so mote it be*
> *With these words, this spell I cast*

I will this magic to act fast

The words don't have to be complicated or scholarly. As long as the incantation meets your intention, and you continue to visualize your goal, the spell will act accordingly.

Now that you have the intention, ingredients, and incantation, how do you put it all together?

The actions of the spell are simple. Remember, when working with candles, you want to cleanse them first. Then you'll want to anoint your candle with the Patchouli oil. Anointing is also when you will say your incantation for the first time.

To anoint your candle, put a drop of patchouli oil on your forefinger; starting at the top of your candle, anoint down until you reach the middle of the candle. Put another drop of oil on your forefinger and start from the bottom of the candle, anointing up until you reach the middle of your candle. The two streaks of oil will meet in the middle.

This is the anointing method for spells you are using to attract something to you, in this case, money.

Once the candle is anointed, set it on your altar and light the candle. Say your incantation three times willfully and strongly, visualizing your goal and then extinguish the candle. Repeat the burning and incanting steps for three consecutive nights and then bury the remaining candle stub outside.

Now, when you go to actually write your spell down in a Book of Shadows or Grimoire, it might end up looking more like this.

Spell to Attract Money

Supplies:
> Green candle
> Patchouli oil

Instructions:
- Open/Cast Sacred Circle
- Cleanse green candle
- Anoint the candle with patchouli oil while visualizing your goal, and say this incantation:

Bring more money to me
This is my will, so mote it be
With these words, this spell I cast
I will this magic to act fast

- Set your candle on the altar and light the candle.
- Repeat the incantation three times.
- Extinguish the candle.
- Close the circle.
- Repeat the burning and incanting steps for three consecutive nights.
- Bury the remaining candle stub outside.

- Continue to visualize your goal after your spell is cast.

You may notice that a lot of spells call for papers to be folded in thirds or incantations repeated three times. Three is a powerful magical number and is used frequently in spells to enhance their power.

However, you will find it easiest to write your spells out so that you can refer back to them and know that what they mean is fine. Writing spells can be fun and empowering, and they get you to think creatively about your Wiccan lifestyle. Even if you don't think you'll be interested, you are encouraged to at least give it a try.

Chapter Four: Spells for Friendship

As you start to work with spells and begin to cast, and possibly write your own spell, you will begin to see how varied the spells and their ingredients can be. Just because a spell is simple, it doesn't mean that it is less effective. The power comes from you and your intention!

Spells that deal with friendship encompass several subcategories of sorts. In this chapter, you will discover spells for attracting new friends. There will be spells to help friends, strengthen friendships, peacefully end friendships, find an animal companion or familiar, resolve conflict with friends, and other similar topics.

If any of the spells cover working on a specific friend, such as helping a friend pass a test or helping them find their lost wallet, remember that you should have their expressed permission before casting the spell.

Friends can come in many forms. Sometimes, they are people, animals, or even natural objects, such as trees or rocks. Humans are social animals, and loneliness is a terrible feeling. It can be hard to connect with other people. Friendships change as people grow and move and change. Sometimes, friends pass away or move away, and this can leave a void.

There are many emotions and circumstances that involve friends. The spells in this chapter are going to touch on several situations that can be encountered with existing friends or in the pursuit of new friends.

Sometimes, spells are stronger when cast by two Wiccans. Included in the spells below are a few friendship spells designed to be cast with a friend, ideally, another practicing Wiccan.

Blessing a Friend

Cast this spell at the Full Moon to bless a friend.

Supplies:
    White Candle
    Blessed or Holy Oil
    Paper and Pen or Personal Item of Friend

Instructions:
- Get friend's permission to cast this spell, and use a personal item of theirs in the spell.
- Cast a Sacred Circle.
- Cleanse the white candle
- Carve friend's name or personal symbols on the wax of the candle.
- Anoint the candle with blessing oil.
- Set the candle on the altar, on top of a piece of paper with their name or beside a personal item that belongs to this friend.
- Burn a portion of the candle every day for 7 consecutive days.
- While the candle is burning, say this incantation:
    [Friend's Name] you are blessed. May good things come to you and may you be free of negativity and harm. Your heart is full of

light. May your journeys be safe, may you remain healthy, and may your mind stay strong. You are blessed.

- Close the Circle.
- After seven days, bury the remaining candle stub.
- Write down the incantation for your friend to keep if they wish.

Attracting a New Friend

Cast this spell during the Waxing Moon to attract new friends to you.

Supplies:
>Three brown candles
>Blank paper and pen
>Heatproof dish

Instructions:
- Open the Sacred Circle.
- Light three brown candles on your altar.
- On the blank paper, write down a list of attributes you'd like in a friend. Be as detailed as possible. Include personality traits, physical features, and any historical or background information you want them to have or relate to. Visualize them clearly as they are written and spoken.
- As you write your list, speak each item aloud.
- Fold your paper three times.
- Light the edge on one of the candle flames.
- Put the burning paper in your heatproof dish.
- While the paper burns, say this incantation:
>*With heart and mind, I speak*
>*Draw to me the one I seek*
>*Let this list be their guide*
>*To bring this friend to my side*
>*Pain and loneliness will be no more*
>*Bring an ally to my door*
>*With pleasures great and sorrows few*
>*We shall build this friendship new*
>*With my words, this spell is done*
>*Do as ye will and harm ye none*
- Let the paper burn out.
- Close the circle.
- Scatter the ash to the wind.
- Continue to visualize and imagine the friend that you seek entering your life.

Hearing From a Friend You Miss

Cast this spell during a Waxing Moon to encourage communication from a friend that you miss and have not heard from recently.

Supplies:
    Blank paper
    Black pen
    White candle
    Heatproof dish

Instructions:
- Open a circle.
- Cleanse the white candle and then light it on your altar.
- By candlelight, write a letter to a friend that you miss or have not heard from in a while. As you write the letter, visualize how you would feel when they contacted you. Think of how you miss them, and try to remember the last time you saw them in person or the last time you spoke to them.
- When your letter is written, fold it in half three times.
- Say this incantation three times:
    From you, I wish to hear
    You may be far, but I feel you near
    Do harm to none
    This spell is done

- Light the letter on the white candle, and let burn in a heatproof dish to release it into the universe, or send the letter to your friend for a more direct approach.
- Close the circle.

Friendship Knot

Cast this spell as a charm to draw a new friend into your life. It is best to cast during a Waxing Moon.

Supplies:
> White string, 12 inches
> Gray string, 12 inches
> Pink string, 12 inches
> Blank paper and pen

Instructions:
- Cast a sacred circle.
- Take a moment to meditate on why you are seeking a new friend. Write the reason down on your blank paper. This part is important as understanding your desire for a new friend can better help you connect with the right kind of friend you currently need.
- Next, write a list of the 12 most important traits you would like your new friend to have. Speak the traits aloud and clearly visualize them.
- Hold your three strings together, and for each trait, tie a knot in the strings. Space them about 1 inch apart.
- As you tie a knot, speak aloud the trait that it represents.
- Close the circle.
- Wear your charm as a bracelet or necklace, or tie it to your keychain or purse.
- Periodically touch your charm and visualize the chosen traits again.
- Keep it on your person until a new friend enters your life.

Dream Pet Spell

Cast this spell during the Waxing Moon to attract an animal companion to you.

Supplies:
> Small container with lid (jar, bottle, etc.)
> Water
> Blank paper and pen
> Artistic tools (optional)
> Object representing animal you want

Instructions:
- Open a Sacred Circle.
- On a blank paper, draw the type of pet you want. Be as detailed and artistic as you want, adding color and minor details if you like. (Please keep in mind that magic has limits; stick to animals that are known to exist, and try to keep to pets that are legal or can be easily acquired in your geographical region).
- Underneath your drawing, list characteristics you would like your pet to have. Include physical traits, personality traits, and any quirks or special traits you want them to have.
- Strongly visualize your animal companion and speak the traits aloud.
- Fold the paper three times and say this incantation three times:

An animal companion I desire
This pet, please help me acquire
Let us form a lasting trust
Harm none is a must

- Fill the container up with water, leaving a little room at the top
- Add an object that relates to your desired pet (a ball for a dog, milk for a cat, grass for a horse, a branch for a bird, etc.).
- Finally, place the folded paper in the container of water with the animal object
- Close the lid on the container.
- Close your circle.
- Set the container somewhere you think your pet would enjoy. Give the water time to dissolve the paper and continue to visualize your ideal animal companion.

Repair a Friendship

Cast this spell during the Waxing Moon to help repair a friendship. Whether you've had a fight, disagreement, or falling out, this spell will help you to reach a resolution.

Supplies:
>Pink candle
>Blank paper and pen
>Envelope
>Material to make a gift for your friend

Instructions:
- Open the Sacred Circle.
- Cleanse the pink candle.
- Carve a symbol for friendship on the wax of the pink candle.
- Carve additional symbols for peace or love on the candle if you wish.
- Light the candle and meditate for a few moments on the disagreement that you had with your friend.
- Visualize a mended friendship, and say this incantation:
  >*Two friends have had a fight*
  >*Please help to set this right*
  >*Help us to remain friends*
  >*Let us make amends*
- At the top of the blank paper, draw the symbols you carved into the candle. Then begin to write down your feelings about repairing the friendship. If there is anything you would like to apologize for or accept responsibility for, write that down. Write down what you would like to happen with this friendship, as well as the reasons you want to remain friends.
- Sign your name on the paper.
- Make a small yet thoughtful gift for your friend.
- While making the gift, continue to visualize a mended friendship and your overall desires for this spell.
- Put the gift and the paper inside the envelope and seal the envelope with wax from the pink candle.
- Close the circle.
- When you next see your friend, give them the envelope.

Spell for Everlasting Friendship

At the Full Moon, cast this spell with a friend you wish to keep in your life forever.

Supplies:
  2 glass jars or bottles with lids
  Dried Apple Blossom petals
  Dried Pink Rose petals
  White sugar
  White Candle
  Red Candle

Instructions:
- Open the Sacred Circle.
- Cleanse the white and red candles.
- Light the candles on your altar.
- Stand with your friend before the altar, and take a jar or bottle each.
- Fill the jars with a combination of the flower petals, and top off with a handful of white sugar.
- While filling your jars, imagine the jar filled with love, friendship, and longevity. Visualize a strong, lasting friendship and how it will look when you are still friends years and years from now. Add trust, forgiveness, loyalty, and kindness for your friend into the jar.

- Put the lids on the jars and say this incantation together:
    Most friendships come and grow
    Please allow ours to always grow
    By our will, so mote it be
    Friends forever, times three
- After the incantation, exchange friendship jars with each other.
- Blow out the candles.
- Close the circle.
- Keep your respective jars in your bedrooms or personal space.

Protection for a Friend

Cast this spell at the Full or Waning Moon to provide a friend with protection.

Supplies:
> Picture of friend or personal object
> White candle
> Light blue candle

Instructions:
- Get a friend's expressed permission before casting a spell on their behalf.
- Cast a Sacred Circle.
- Cleanse white and light blue candles
- Light candles and set image of a friend or personal object in between the two candles.
- Visualize a strong protective barrier around your friend.
- Make sure it is a barrier for protection against physical harm and psychic harm.
- Say this incantation three times while holding the protective barrier visualization:
  > *Protection for (friend's name) is my desire*
  > *Please grant them strength and courage of fire*
  > *Keep them safe from harm to body and mind*
  > *This protection spell I bind*
  > *Do harm to none*
  > *This spell is done*
- Re-visualize that protective barrier for your friend.
- Blow out the candles.
- Close the circle.
- Burn the candles and repeat incanting for three consecutive nights.
- Bury the remaining candle stubs outside.

Finding Forgiveness

During the Waning Moon, cast this spell to receive forgiveness from a friend.

Supplies:
> White candle
> Lavender incense

Instructions:
- Open the Sacred Circle.
- Cleanse the white candle.
- On the altar, light the white candle and the lavender incense.
- Meditate, deeply breathing in the scent and smoke of the incense.
- Visualize yourself receiving forgiveness and being forgiven.
- Repeat this incantation three times:
  > *To err is human*
  > *To forgive is transcendent*
  > *Please grant me forgiveness*
  > *I seek release and independence*
- Return to a meditative state while visualizing yourself receiving forgiveness and being forgiven.
- Blow out the candle.

- Close the circle.
- Repeat the candle burning, meditation, and incanting for seven consecutive days.

Peacefully End a Friendship

During the Waning Moon, cast this spell to amicably break a friendship bond that no longer serves you.

Supplies:
   An object that represents the friendship (friendship bracelet; a gift from them)
   A bowl of dirt or sand

Instructions:
- Open the Sacred Circle.
- On the altar, bury the friendship object in the bowl of dirt or sand. Completely cover the item, so it can't be seen at all.
- Repeat this incantation at least three times, more if your intuition tells you to:
   Tonight, I banish this toxic bond
   Under the waning moon and beyond
   Let us both retreat on peaceful terms
   Harm none, this I confirm
- Visualize the friendship ending on amicable terms. Think of your friend and why they no longer fit into your life. Give a silent thanks for their friendship and wish them well without you in their life.
- Close the circle.
- Repeat incantation over a burred object as frequently as you feel the need.
- Once the friendship is ended, bury the dirt or sand and the friendship object outside far away from home, work, or school.

Friendship Potion (Drinkable)

During the days of the Waxing Moon, prepare and cast this spell to attract new friendships.

Supplies:
Drink pitcher
Water
Strawberries
Lemon Juice
Fresh Mint Leaves

Instructions:
- A day before you want to cast the spell cut the strawberries. Fill the pitcher with cold water, and then add the strawberries. Keep it in the refrigerator overnight.
- Cast your sacred circle.
- Take 1 cup of the strawberry water in a cup.
- Add one drop of lemon juice to the strawberry water at the beginning of each line of the incantation.
- Say this incantation:
  Earth, water, fire, air
  Send to me a friend who cares
  Please bring me a kindred soul

Two halves make a friendship whole
Through good and bad a friendship keeps
This is my will, so mote it be

- Stir the strawberry water and lemon juice together. Stir in a clockwise direction
- Garnish the drink with fresh mint.
- Drink your drink and visualize a new friend entering your life.
- Drink slowly and imagine all the details and qualities that you want in a new friend.
- When the glass is empty, spend a few moments meditating on your new friend at your altar.
- Close the circle.
- Repeat spell with the remaining the strawberry water one cup at a time.

Find an Animal Totem or Guide

Cast this spell on a Full Moon night to find your animal guide. Cast this spell just before you go to sleep.

Supplies:
>Book of Shadows or Grimoire
>Pen
>White candle

Instructions:
- Cast your Sacred Circle.
- Cleanse the white candle.
- Light the candle on your altar and open your Grimoire or Book of Shadows to a blank page for a journal entry.
- Write this incantation in your Grimoire or Book of Shadows:
  >*Guardians of my dreams, open mine eyes wide*
  >*Lead me to my spirit protector and guide*
  >*Show me the magical path to walk*
  >*So that we may communicate and talk*
- Meditate on that incantation while the white candle burns low. Visualize yourself finding your animal totem and guide.
- Blow out the candle.
- Close your circle.
- Sleep with your Book of Shadows next to your bed, and write down any details from dreams you have as soon as you wake up.
- Your dreams will guide you to your spirit animal. Spirit animals can be very useful on your Wiccan path.

Strengthen a Friendship

Cast this spell on the Full Moon to strengthen the bond you have with a friend.

Supplies:
  Brown Candle
  Yellow paper
  Pen
  Heatproof container

Instructions:
- Open your Sacred Circle.
- Cleanse the candle.
- Carve symbols of friendship into the candle and light it on your altar.
- Draw your friendship symbols on the yellow paper. Write words you associate with friendship and words you associate with the friend whom you are looking to strengthen the relationship with.
- Visualize the two of you growing closer together and forming a stronger friendship bond.
- Fold the yellow paper three times and write, 'Harm None' on the outside of the paper.

- Light the yellow paper from the brown candle flame.
- Transfer the paper to the heatproof dish and allow it to burn.
- Keep visualizing your strengthened friendship bond until the paper burns out.
- Close the circle.
- Disperse paper ash into the wind.

Finding a True Friend

During the Waxing Moon, cast this spell to find a true, loyal, lifelong friend.

Supplies:
> Pink candle
> Candle of your favorite color
> Sandalwood essential oil
> Pink string
> String of your favorite color

Instructions:
- Open your Sacred Circle.
- Cleanse both candles.
- Anoint the candle that is your favorite color with sandalwood oil and say:
  > *With all my individuality*
  > *This candle now represents me*
- Anoint the pink candle with the sandalwood oil and say:
  > *With all their individuality*
  > *This candle now represents a friend's personality*
- Light both candles on your altar and say this incantation:
  > *I draw a friend to me, loyal and true*
  > *By the loving power of two*
  > *Our bond will grow strong and tight*
  > *By both our wills, sealed by candlelight*
- Blow both candles out.
- Use the two colored strings to tie the candles together, visualizing a new friend coming into your life. Visualize details in personality or appearance that you want this friend to have.
- Close the circle.
- Leave the bound candles on your altar until a new friend enters your life.

Friendship Bag

This charm is best to cast during a Waxing Moon to help attract new friends.

Supplies:
Orange or yellow natural fiber fabric
White or yellow string
Yellow or Red rose petals
Penny
Red or yellow crystal or stone

Instructions:
- Open your Sacred Circle.
- Lay the fabric open on your altar; square or circular cut is the easiest shape to work with.
- Put the rose petals in the center of the fabric.
- Hold the crystal or stone in your dominant hand and say this incantation three times:
  Bring to me new friends true
  Bind us together like with glue
  Let our friendship grow strong
  Find us a place to belong
- Set the crystal into the bag, and pick up the penny with your dominant hand.
- Visualize the kinds of friends you want to make, including details for their personalities and even physical appearances. Envision what it will be like to have these friends.
- Kiss the penny for good luck, and add it to the bag.
- Fold the edges of the fabric, and use the colored string to tie the fabric around the ingredients and into a bag.
- Close your circle.
- Carry your charm bag on your person or in a bag.
- Periodically touch the charm bag and give it a squeeze, releasing the magic and visualizing your intended goal.

The spells in this chapter are designed to be an introduction to spellcasting and give you a starting point to play around with spells. Any spells that are pre-written can be altered and adapted as needed for your uses.

Friendships can be complicated, emotional, hard to start, and hard to keep. They can also be enjoyable, everlasting, and strong support systems. In any situation, remember to feel grateful for the solid, good friendships you have and try to remove yourself from toxic friendships.

You can find friends in people, family members, animals, spirits, and other entities. Even a spirit guide or animal totem can become a friend, confidant, and support system as you walk the Wiccan path.

Wicca For Beginners 2021: Part 2,

An Introduction To Wiccan Magic and Rituals

Chapter Five: Spells for Prosperity

Prosperity is defined as being successful. Success can relate to career, personal life, luck, money, wealth, and happiness. Any feelings of abundance and success relate back to prosperity.

Spells can be used to increase personal prosperity. If you applied for a job, casting a spell can help ensure that you land the position! If you are a little short on cash, do a money spell, and get a boost in finances. Are you feeling unlucky? Cast a luck spell!

It is not uncommon for people to hit a period of low prosperity. Usually, this leads to a bummed mood and negative thoughts, which creates more animosity toward the already tense situation. Fortunately, as a Wiccan, you have the power to change your energy to a more positive vibe, as well as influence the universe to give you a little hand!

This chapter is going to cover spells regarding jobs, interviews, and careers. It will also go over spells that have to do with money, riches, finances, and wealth. There will be spells concerning happiness and luck, too.

Money Bath

Cast this spell during the Waxing Moon to attract more money.

      Supplies:
         Green ribbons
         Patchouli oil

Instructions:
- In your bathroom, create a sacred, safe space to cast your spell with your intentions.
- Tie the green ribbons around the bathtub faucet.
- Start filling the tub, allowing the water to run over the ribbons.
- Add 3-5 drops of Patchouli oil to the bathwater.
- Once the tub is filled, soak in your money bath.
- While you soak, visualize money in different forms. Visualize yourself gaining money. Visualize yourself attracting money.
- You are 'soaking up' the money.

Good Luck Business Charm

This spell is most effective when cast during the Waxing Moon. Use it to bring luck into your business.

     Supplies:
          Dried bay leaves
          Green ribbon or string
          3 gold or bronze coins
          Blank paper

Instructions:
- Open the Sacred Circle.
- On your altar, crumple up the piece of paper to make it pliable.
- Open the paper back up, and in the cent, put the bay leaves and coins at the center.
- Use the green ribbon or string to tie the paper into a parcel.
- Hold the charm in your dominant hand and spend 5 to 10 minutes meditating on your business goals. Visualize your business goals and desires.
- Keep the charm at your work desk or in your office.

Perfect Career Spell

Cast this spell during the New Moon or Waxing Moon to help land yourself the perfect career for yourself!

Supplies:
- Green candle
- Basil or Sage oil
- Sage or Patchouli incense

Instructions:
- Cast your Sacred Circle.
- Cleanse the green candle.
- Carve your name into the candle and anoint the candle with the selected oil.
- On your altar, light the candle and incense.
- Meditate to the burning candle, visualizing yourself in a career you love. Really use your imagination to create the perfect career and work environment for yourself in this visualization.
- Say this incantation three times:

  I ask the universe to please guide me to the perfect career for me and my lifestyle
  May the Goddess and God lead me to the path that is designed for my talents
  I am ready to receive this ideal job and career
  Humbly, I ask that my desire come to fruition
  This is my will, so mote it be

- Blow out the green candle.
- Close the circle.

Money Growth Spell

This spell best works during the Waxing Moon to increase your financial status.

   Supplies:
      Healthy house plant
      A silver coin
      Dried patchouli

Instructions:
- Cast a Sacred Circle.
- Set the plant on your altar and sprinkle the patchouli herb around the planet in a deosil (clockwise) circle onto the soil in the plant pot.
- Hold the coin vertically and push it down into the soil so that the edge is sticking out of the dirt.
- Whenever extra money comes your way, take the coin out of the pot and spend it.
- Replace that coin with a new one until the next time money comes your way.

Triple Stone Luck Spell

Cast this spell during the Waxing Moon to increase your luck.

Supplies:
: 3 crystals
: Green candle
: Frankincense incense
: Blank paper
: Green pen
: Wooden box

Instructions:
- Cast your Sacred Circle.
- Cleanse the green candle.
- Light the candle and the incense.
- Then place your hands over the wooden box and say this incantation:
  Earth, air, water, fire
  Luck is my heart's desire
  This box I fix for this spell
  Keep my heart very well
- On the paper, write about a positive instance in your life when you felt very lucky. Really visualize the event as you write it out.
- Roll the paper up, and put it in your box.
- One by one, hold the gemstones in your dominant hand.
- Say this incantation for each one:
  Please send Luck my way
- One by one, place each stone in the spell box.
- Extinguish the green candle.
- Close your circle.
- For three consecutive nights, light the candle, open the box and read your paragraph aloud. Continue to visualize this event. Then hold each stone individually in your dominant hand and ask to be sent luck. Then put the paper and stones back in the box.
- After the third night, open the box for exactly 1 hour to release the magical energy.
- Whenever you think you need a little extra luck, carry the three crystals with you.

Frog of Prosperity Spell

This spell should be cast during the Waxing Moon to increase prosperity.

Supplies:
Frog charm (something that can fit in your pocket)
Gold coins
Sand
Money Powder (Mix 1 cup sugar with a pinch of basil, cinnamon, mint, and nutmeg)
Plate

Instructions:
- Open a sacred circle.
- Set the plate on your altar, and put the coins on the plate.
- Set the frog on top of the coins.
- Sprinkle the frog and coins with the sand and the Money Powder.
- Close the circle.
- Set the plate under your bed, with the frog facing the door of your bedroom.
- Every morning, sprinkle a little more sand and money powder on the frog and coins.
- Each night before bed, stare at the frog and visualize money coming into your life
- Hold onto the money visualization as you go to bed.

Abundance Bag

Cast this spell during the Waxing Moon.

> Supplies:
>> Green candle
>> Green cloth, natural fiber
>> Gold string or ribbon
>> Wheat
>> Corn meal
>> Cinnamon
>> Chamomile
>> Ground ginger
>> Lavender

Instructions:
- Cast a Sacred Circle.
- Cleanse the green candle.
- Light the green candle and chant this incantation three times:
  > *Goddess and God, please grant me abundance*
  > *This I ask of you*
  > *Here in this hour*
  > *Please lend me power*
- As you chant, visualize yourself achieving the levels of success and abundance that you desire. Whether it is wealth, career success, or luck, imagine yourself getting it.
- Place the green cloth flat on your altar.
- Combine a pinch of each of the herbal ingredients into the center of the cloth.
- Bundle the cloth up into a parcel and tie it closed with the golden string.
- Seal the knot with some green candle wax.
- Hold the bundle in your dominant hand and say:
  > *Bundled abundance by candlelight*
  > *Bound with wax and tied tight*
  > *Please grant me the abundance I desire*
  > *My will is spoken by candle fire*
- Set the sachet back on your altar, and allow yourself to bask in the candlelight while continuing to visualize your desired abundance.
- Close the circle.
- Leave the sachet on your altar and for three consecutive nights, light the green candle, and repeat your prayer to the Goddess and God.

- Carry the sachet with you after the three consecutive nights, or set it in a place that corresponds to your goal and intention.

Luck Oil

Mix this oil during the Waxing Moon and wear to attract luck.

       Supplies:
           2 oz glass bottle with lid
           1/8 c carrier oil (almond oil, apricot oil, jojoba oil)
           5 drops wintergreen oil
           5 drops vanilla oil or extract
           5 drops cinnamon oil
           1 tsp vegetable glycerin (optional)

Instructions:
- Cast the Sacred Circle.
- In a bowl, mix the three herbal oils together with the vegetable glycerin (if using).
- Once the scented oils are mixed thoroughly, add in the carrier oil and mix well.
- Pour the combined oils into the glass jar. Screw the lid on and shake well to mix even more.
- As you are mixing the oils together, visualize yourself being lucky, or imagine symbols that you associate with luck.
- Close the circle.

- Any time you feel like you want to attract a little luck (whether you seek money, a job, or a specific outcome in a situation), dab a few drops of the Luck Oil on your wrists, heart chakra, and third eye chakra (center of your chest and forehead).

Prosperity Jar

This spell is best cast during the Waxing Moon to increase your personal prosperity.

Supplies:
> Glass jar with lid (such as a mason jar)
> Silver coins
> Basil or Patchouli essential oil
> Lemongrass
> Thyme
> Rosemary
> Basil
> Bay leaves
> Cloves
> Cinnamon sticks
> Lavender

Instructions:
- Cast a Sacred Circle.
- Hold your empty jar in both hands. Visualize what personal prosperity looks like to you. Pour luck, wealth, happiness, abundance, and prosperity into the empty jar with your visualizations.
- Put the cinnamon sticks in your jar, up to three of them. Depending on the size of the jar, you may need to cut or break them.
- Next, add equal parts of the remaining dried herbs. Portions vary depending on the size of the jar.
- Put the lid on the jar, and give a little shake to blend the herbs together.
- Continue to visualize your personal prosperity as you mix the herbs and shake your jar.
- Take the lid off again and add up to nine silver coils to your herb mix.
- Next, drip 5-9 drops of the basil or patchouli oil into your jar.
- Screw the lid on again and shake the jar, reinforcing your visualization of personal prosperity.
- If you want to raise its power, hum or chant a little while shaking and mixing the ingredients in the prosperity jar.
- Close your circle.
- Keep your prosperity jar under your bed. On a New Moon, take the jar out and re-visualize personal prosperity while shaking the jar, then place it back under the bed. Repeat this on another New Moon, as many New Moons as you'd like.

Four Elements for Wealth

Cast this spell during the Waxing Moon to attract money.

Supplies:
>Rock salt
>Rain water or Sea water
>Green candle
>Patchouli, Sage, or Basil incense
>Chalice or Goblet
>Libation dish

Instructions:
- Open your Sacred Circle.
- Cleanse the green candle.
- Light the candle and say:
  >*May Firelight my path to wealth*
- Light the incense and say:
  >*May riches float to me on the wind*
- Pour the water into the chalice and say:
  >*May water carry abundance to me on waves*
- Stir the rock salt in the libation dish and say:
  >*May the fertility of earth grow my fortune*
- Meditate on wealth and attracting money and abundance while the candle and the incense burn out. Strongly visualize your desire and intent.

- Close the circle.
- Leave the elements on your altar until you find your fortune changing.

Job Spell

Cast this spell during the New Moon or the Waxing Moon for greater success.

Supplies:
> Green candle
> Rosemary oil

Instructions:
- Open a Sacred Circle.
- Cleanse the green candle.
- Dress the green candle with rosemary oil, and then place it on your altar, lighting it.
- Meditate on the candle, visualizing yourself getting the job you want. Hold a strong image of what that looks like and keep holding that image.
- Close the circle.
- On the night before a job interview, light and burn the candle again, continuing the visualization of you getting that job.

Seven Day Luck Spell

Cast this spell during the Waxing Moon with at least seven days before the full moon.

Supplies:
      Black candle (one that can burn for 7 consecutive nights for the spell)
      Spring or rain water
      Dish/Bowl
      Paper and pen

Instructions:
- Cast the Sacred Circle.
- Cleanse your black 7-day candle.
- Pour the water into your dish, just enough to cover the entire bottom.
- On the piece of paper, write what you desire (job, love, success, money, happiness, etc.).
- Fold the paper three times and set it in the dish of water.
- Set the black candle on top of the paper in the dish and light it.
- Meditate on the candle, truly visualizing what it is you want. Imagine it as though it has already come to pass, and you've already gained your desires.
- Close the circle.
- For seven consecutive nights, before going to sleep, open your circle, light the candle, and continue to visualize what you wrote on the paper. Then close the circle and go to sleep.

- After the seventh night, take the paper and the candle stub, and bury them together in the ground.

Silver Prosperity Spell

Cast this spell under the light of the Full Moon.

Supplies:
- Cauldron
- Seven fresh Basil leaves
- Rain or spring water
- Silver coin

Instructions:
- Cast the Sacred Circle.
- Set the cauldron on your altar, and put the silver coin on the bottom of the cauldron.
- Pour your water over the coin in the cauldron, at least halfway full.
- Take your cauldron to a window, and set it in the moonlight.
- One at a time, drop the basil leaves into the water, and say this incantation three times:

  By this Full Moon
  Bless me with prosperity soon
  Silver in water shines
  Let wealth become mine

- Leave the cauldron in the moonlight overnight.
- Close the circle.
- The next morning, pour water and basil outside and carry the coin on your person.

Abundance by Candlelight Spell

This spell is best cast during the Waxing Moon for success.

Supplies:
> Green candle
> Vanilla oil or extract
> Cinnamon oil
> Large silver coin

Instructions:
- Cast the Sacred Circle.
- Cleanse the green candle.
- Carve the word 'wealth' on the side of the candle and cave symbols relating to money and success that have personal meaning to you.
- Anoint the candle with the cinnamon and vanilla oils.
- Set the coin in the bottom of the candle holder that you plan to burn the candle in. Place the candle on top and light it.
- Let the candle burn down completely, meditating on wealth, prosperity, and abundance. Fully visualize and imagine your goals and intentions.
- Close the circle.
- Keep the wax-covered coin on your person until you welcome more abundance into your life.

Make a Fortune Candle

This DIY spell is best cast during the Waxing Moon or on the Full Moon.

Supplies:
> Green candle wax
> Candle wicks
> 5 round, open glass jar (for candle mold)
> 5 copper coins
> Dried basil and pine needles
> Mortar and pestle
> Double boiler

Instructions:
- Set a sacred space intention in your kitchen.
- In a double boiler on the stovetop, melt the candle wax.
- In the bottom of the candle molds, set one of the copper coins. Place the candle wicks on top of the coins inside the molds.
- Use the mortar and pestle to grind the basil and pine needles together in a fine powder.
- Once the candle wax melts, mix the powdered herbs into the wax.
- Remove the wax from the stovetop and before it cools, pour the wax into the molds over the coin and around the wicks.
- During the process of making your candles, keep visualizing the money you want to make. You can visualize how you want to make money or being surrounded by heaps of money.
- Close your sacred space.
- Allow the candle wax ample time to cool. Use these candles in other money and abundance rituals, or burn them on their own to increase your finances.

Personal prosperity can come in many forms. When you are seeking to improve your own success, remember that you need to define success for yourself. Do you feel successful based on the money you have or make? Is success found in happiness for you? What is your prosperity?

Once you know your own desires when it comes to prosperity and success, you can cast spells aligned with what you truly want. When you work magic based on your wants and desires, the spells are enhanced by your personal power, and you'll find that visualization is easier.

Finding your own success and prosperity is empowering. That doesn't mean you can't invoke your Wiccan power to help things along, especially when it comes to money and financial troubles. Find your personal prosperity and good luck!

Success Oil

Start this spell on a New Moon, and continue it until the next New Moon.

Supplies:
Glass bottle with cork or screw top
5 oz carrier oil (jojoba oil, apricot oil, almond oil, etc.)
Mortar and pestle
1 teaspoon dried Bay
1 teaspoon Vetiver
1 teaspoon Frankincense gum
1 teaspoon Sandalwood oil

Ingredients:
- Open a Sacred Circle.
- Pour carrier oil into the glass bottle, and add the sandalwood oil. Put the top on, and shake the bottle to blend the oils.
- Using the mortar and pestle, grind the frankincense gum and then mash together with the bay leaves and Vetiver.
- When the herbs are thoroughly ground and blended, add the powdered mix to the oil blend.
- Put the lid back on the bottle and shake well.

- Visualize your success and what it means to you to be successful.
- As you shake and visualize, say this incantation three times:
  Mother Goddess and Father God
  Please bless me with success
  Fill this oil with light and joy
  For this task, you I employ
- Close the circle.
- Store the jar of oil in a cool, dark place.
- Once a week, shake the bottle again, repeating your incantation and visualizing success for yourself.
- When the next New Moon comes, strain the oil. Keep the oil and discard the herb bits appropriately.
- To ensure success, wear a dab of the Success Oil on your wrists, heart chakra, and third eye chakra (center of your chest and forehead).
- Wear as frequently as you would like.

Chapter Six: Spells for Romance

Love and romance are popular topics in the Wiccan community, especially for younger and newer practitioners. Love is a powerful force in the universe. It makes up everything in one way or another. Love is universal. Whether it is love for yourself, love for a friend, love for family, romantic love, love for a child, love for a place, or love for a deity, love is universal.

This chapter is primarily focused on romantic love; however, not every spell falls into that category. Whenever you are working magic, especially love spells, it is important to remember not to cast spells directly on another person without their prior expressed permission.

Love spells, especially, are considered manipulative and potentially dangerous. If the spell works too well, the other person could become obsessed. If the spell is cast on someone you don't know well, they may end up treating you terribly. Furthermore, casting spells on others is a direct violation of the Wiccan creed 'An Harm None, do as You Will.'

Everyone knows what it is like to have a crush or be in love with someone who doesn't return those feelings, who doesn't know about those feelings, or who doesn't even know who you are. It can be painful and confusing.

Love can also be amazing and wonderful. It can be a huge source of happiness, support, and salvation. Romantic love can create a bond and connection with another person who provides you with the fulfillment you've never imagined.

More important than romantic love is self-love. Wicca teaches about self-love, too, and you should always strive for self-love before seeking love from someone else.

Full Moon Love Spell

Cast this spell on the Full Moon to attract love.

> Supplies:
>> Moonstones
>> Basil oil
>> Cinnamon oil
>> Red candle
>> Pen and blank paper
>> Heatproof dish

Instructions:
- Cast a Sacred Circle.
- Cleanse the red candle.
- Dress your candle with the two herbal oils. Visualize love and being loved as you anoint the candles.
- Light the candle and continue to visualize love and love symbols.
- On the paper, draw some symbols that stand for love, and write words that mean love to you. Write your own name on the paper and connect a line from each word and symbol back to your name.
- Fold the paper three times.
- Say this incantation:
  > *Upon this blessed night*
  > *Unite two souls by candlelight*
  > *To the Goddess I beseech thee*
  > *Bring me romance, turn me into we*
- Set your moonstone in the heatproof dish, and light the corner of the paper on the red candle flame.
- Transfer the burning paper to the heatproof dish on top of the moonstone.
- Say this incantation three times as the paper burns:
  > *By Moon and Stone, I draw in love*
  > *I ask for blessings from above*
  > *Bring me a lover all mine*
  > *I extend my gratitude to the divine*
- Keep visualizing the love you want, and let the candle burn out.
- Close your circle.
- The next morning, after the moon has set, dispose of the paper ash.
- Keep the moonstone as a charm until a new love enters your life.

Love Pouch

Cast this spell during the Waxing Moon or Full Moon.

Supplies:
> Pink cloth, made of natural fibers
> Pink or red string
> 2 tablespoons pink flower petals
> 1 tablespoon dried anise stars
> 1 tablespoon cinnamon chips
> Blank sheet of paper, about 2 in by 2 in
> Red pen and Red marker

Instructions:
- Cast Sacred Circle.
- On the pink cloth, draw two overlapping hearts with the red marker.
- On the blank paper, write as many qualities as you'd like in a romantic partner. Be as specific as you want, and say each word aloud, visualizing the type of person you want to attract.
- Fold the paper three times and set it in the center of the cloth.
- Add the herbs to the cloth overtop the paper. Continue to visualize what you want as you add the herbs.
- Sat this incantation three times:
  > *Goddess of Love, I call to thee*
  > *Bring the love I dream to me*
  > *With my wish, I bind this spell*
  > *Make sure none are harmed as well*
- Bind the bag with the string and tie it into a pouch.
- Close the circle.
- Carry your Love Pouch with you throughout the day, visualize the love you are trying to attract, and give the bag a squeeze to release the magical power.

Draw in Love

Start casting this spell two nights before the Full Moon. The last night that you work the spell should be the Full Moon.

        Supplies:
                Silver ring, for finger
                Metal bowl
                Moonlight Water (water that has sat out under a full moon with a quartz crystal bathing in it)

Instructions:
- Open Sacred Circle.
- Set the metal bowl on your altar and place the silver ring in the bottom.
- Next, fill the bowl with Moonlight Water.
- Set the bowl in a window where the moon shines in.
- Visualize the traits of a lover you want to attract.
- Say this incantation over the bowl three times:
	Mother Goddess, silver and true
	Send light forth from you
	Swiftly as the changing side

Send a lover to my side

- Close the circle.
- Repeat the incantation for the next two nights, ending on the Full Moon.
- Once the spell is complete, wear the silver ring on your finger or a chain around your neck until a new love enters your life.

Thanks for Love

Cast this spell during the Waxing Moon to express your gratitude to the Goddess and God for a love you have or had in your life.

Supplies:
> White candle
> 2 pink roses
> Athame

Instructions:
- Open a Sacred Circle.
- Cleanse the white candle.
- With the Athame, carve a personal symbol on the candle for both yourself and the other person you are honoring.
- Light the candle and set one rose on each side to represent you and your lover or former lover.
- Say this incantation:
    > *Thank you, Goddess, for my love*
    > *Thank you for this gift from above*
    > *Thank you for this love so true*
    > *My heart is full, thanks to you*
- Let the candle burn out, meditating on the relationship that you are thankful for.
- Close the circle.
- Bury the candle stub and the two roses outside.

Love Charm

This spell is most effective when cast during the Waxing Moon.

Supplies:
> Red cloth, made of natural fibers
> Pink string
> 2 rose petals, any color
> 2 lavender sprigs
> 2 yarrow sprigs
> 2 apple seeds
> Blank paper and pen

Instructions:
- Open a Sacred Circle.
- Set the cloth out on your altar, and place all the herbs at the center of it. You can use fresh or dried herbs for this spell.
- On the blank paper, write this incantation:
    > *Find me a lover who is right for me*
    > *In every way. Find a lover for me*
    > *Who I am right for in every way*
- While writing, visualize your goal and intention of finding the right love for you
- Fold the paper three times, and set it on top of the herbs.
- Use the pink string to tie the sachet.

- Close the circle.
- Sleep with the sachet under your pillow until a new love enters your life. Before you go to bed at night, visualize your spell's intention and goal.

Blessed Marriage

This spell can be cast on the New Moon or Full Moon. This spell is designed to be cast on a couple that is already engaged or planning their wedding. It can be cast for a couple you know. If you are casting the spell for another couple, seek permission from them first.

Supplies:
> Pink Candle
> Blue candle
> Rose incense
> Chamomile essential oil

Instructions:
- Open a Sacred Circle.
- Cleanse the two candles.
- Light the rose incense and then anoint both candles with the chamomile oil.
- While anointing the candles, envision a happy, harmonious, and blessed marriage union and relationship after the wedding ceremony.
- Set the candles beside the other and then light them.
- Meditate on the burning candles, and visualize the happy marriage again. Visualize a harmonious living situation and the married couple having fun and happy experiences
- Say this incantation:
  > *Goddess and God*
  > *As you are joined with each other*
  > *Join together these two lovers*
  >
  > *Bring them together in harmony*
  > *Let this be true in their matrimony*
  > *A balanced relationship does this spell make*
  > *Equal give and equal take*
  >
  > *Watch over this relationship*
  > *Foster a truly loving fellowship*
  > *A future of love and bliss*
  > *May they seal this bond with a kiss*
  >
  > *Goddess and God*
  > *I implore thee*
  > *Join this couple in harmony*
- Blow out the candles.

- Meditate on the happy and blessed marriage until the incense burns out.
- Close the circle.

Attract Love Pendant

This spell is best cast during the Waxing Moon.

Supplies:
> Dried rose petals
> Dried chamomile
> Dried lavender
> Small rose quartz
> Pink string
> Pink cord
> Mortar and pestle
> Pendant jar that can be attached to a necklace

Instructions:
- Cast the Sacred Circle.
- Cleanse the candle.
- In the mortar and pestle, combine equal portions of the dried herbs and grind them together into a powder.
- Fill the jar pendant with the herb powder and small pieces of rose quartz
- Close the jar and hold it to your heart chakra (center of your chest), and say this incantation three times:
  > *Goddess grant me love*
  > *True, loyal, and bright*
  > *Someone to fill my heart with light*
  > *Send me a lover true*

This is the wish I ask of you
- Permanently seal it with pink candle wax.
- Use the pink cord to string your pendant and tie three knots in the cord on either side of the jar pendant.
- Close the circle.
- Wear the spell as a necklace until a new lover enters your life.

Fertility Spell

Cast this spell during the Full Moon for the highest potency. This spell is designed to be cast by two people in a relationship who are seeking to have a child. Both partners need to participate in the spell.

Supplies:
>Lock of hair from each person
>Oak tree bark
>White candle
>Glass bowl
>Spring or rain water

Instructions:
- Open your Sacred Circle.
- Cleanse the candle.
- Hold hands with your partner for the duration of the spell.
- One of you should pour water into the glass bowl, while the other should light the white candle.
- Each person places their own lock of hair in the bowl of water.
- Hold the bark in your hand, and stir the bowl of water while saying this incantation three times:
  >*Parents we wish to be*
  >*Bless a child unto me*
  >*When we are ready*
  >*When it is time*
  >*Send us a child, truly divine*
- Kiss the bark and then kiss your partner while passing off the bark to them.
- Your partner will stir the bowl of water and repeat this incantation three times:
  >*Parents we wish to be*
  >*Bless a child unto me*
  >*When we are ready*
  >*When it is time*
  >*Send us a child, truly divine*
- Your partner will kiss the bark and then drop it into the bowl.
- Stand on each side of the bowl, and hold your hands together over the bowl.
- Together say this incantation once:
  >*Parents we wish to be*
  >*Bless a child unto me*
  >*When we are ready*
  >*When it is time*

Send us a child, truly divine

- Close the circle.
- Keep the bowl next to or under your shared bed. Both of you should visualize the goal of your spell every night before going to sleep and especially prior to intimacy.

Lavender Lust Potion

Cast this spell during the Waxing Moon. This spell is designed to increase lust and sexual intimacy for an established couple. Remember to get your partner's prior consent before casting the spell.

Supplies:
> Fresh lavender
> White Wine
> Red candle

Instructions:
- Open a Sacred Circle.
- Cleanse red candle.
- Carve symbols of sex, lust, and desire on the candle.
- Light the candle on your altar, and spend a moment visualizing the intention and desire of your spell.
- Put the fresh lavender into the bottle of wine, and reseal the cap or cork with red candle wax.
- Close the circle.
- Keep the white wine bottle in a cool, dark place for three days and three nights.
- Serve yourself and your partner a glass of the wine to help spark sexual desire.

Love Attraction Bath

Perform this spell during the Waxing Moon to attract love to yourself.

Supplies:
  1 cup Epsom salts
  ½ cup baking soda
  Rose water
  Rose petals
  Ylang-ylang oil
  Chamomile oil
  4-5 red candles

Instructions:
- Set a sacred space and sacred intention in your bathroom.
- Cleanse the red candles and then set them around the bathroom for proper lighting.
- Mix the Epsom salts and baking soda together.
- Add in 3-5 drops each of the herbal oils and the rose water.
- Sprinkle the bottom of the tub with the bath salts mix.
- Toss in a handful of rose petals.
- Light the candles and turn down the lights.
- Fill the tub with warm water.
- Soak in the bath, and visualize the intention of your spell.
- Try to imagine the kind of lover you want and the type of relationship you wish to have with the other person.
- Stay in the tub for as long as you want, fully soaking up the love.

Honey Jar of Love

Cast this spell during the Waxing Moon or on the Full Moon to attract a new lover.

Supplies:
  Mason jar
  1 cup of raw or filtered honey
  Rose petals
  2 Cinnamon sticks
  3 Vanilla beans
  Lavender flowers
  Orange peels
  Blank pink paper and pen
  Envelope
  Red candle

Instructions:
- Open a Sacred Circle.
- Cleanse the red candle.
- Carve symbols of love and attraction on the candle.
- Light your candle, and set the empty jar in the center of your altar.
- First, put the orange peel into the bottom of your jar. Then add the rose petals and the lavender flowers. Next, add the cinnamon sticks and vanilla beans.
- Pour the cup of honey into the jar. Pour in a deosil (clockwise) motion so that the honey drips into the jar, all over the ingredients.

- Write your name in the center of the paper. Around it, write down words to describe the personality and physical traits of a lover you want to attract. Say each trait aloud as you write it.
- Fold the paper three times, and write this incantation on the outside of the paper:
    Goddess of love, to you I pray
    Send me a lover who will always stay
    A love for me, a love for (insert preferred gender)
    Grant me this request
    With love from you, I am blessed
- As you write the incantation, continue to visualize what you want to attract in a lover.
- Put the paper in the envelope, and seal it with red candle wax.
- Use the wax to attach the envelope on the lid of the Mason jar.
- Close the circle
- Screw the lid on the jar, and keep the jar in a cool, dark place until the New Moon
- Remove the jar lid and take out the envelope to bury outside.
- If desired, you can also extract the herbs and bury or leave them in the honey.
- The honey can be used as a sweetener for drinks or toast.

Love Flower Bundles

Cast this spell during the Waxing Moon to draw love to you.

Supplies:
> Daffodils
> Violets
> Roses
> Daisies
> Pink ribbon or string

Instructions:
- Cast Sacred Circle.
- Bundle three of each flower into as many bundles as you wish. Tie each bundle together with the pink ribbon or string.
- Visualize yourself being loved and full of love. Then repeat this incantation three times:
  > *Nature's love, please come to me*
  > *Grant me peace and serenity*
  > *Fill my heart and home with affection*
  > *Send to me a loving connection*
- Close the circle.
- Hang the bundles in windows around your house. The flowers will dry but stay fragrant and decorative.
- Keep the bundles hanging in your windows until you feel more loved and like you are full of love.

Find your Soulmate Spell

Cast this spell during a Waxing Moon or New Moon to help you find your soulmate. This spell is designed for a romantic soulmate.

Supplies:
Red candle
Pink candle
The personal object you can part with
Blank paper and pink or red pen
Envelope
Fairy dust (white sugar, food coloring of any color, and glitter)

Instructions:
- Open the Sacred Circle.
- Cleanse both candles.
- Set the red candle on the left and the pink candle on the right.
- Light both candles.
- On the blank piece of paper, write your name.
- Around your name, draw symbols that make you think of love, passion, eternal love, soulmates, connection, affection, and romance. Write words that correspond to the symbols and their meaning.
- While you are writing, focus and visualize your goal.
- Fold the paper three times and write this incantation:
  To the Goddess and God a pray
  Gift me my soulmate on this day
  With these words, this spell is done
  Always and forever, harm ye none
- Put the paper in the envelope with the personal object.
- Sprinkle some fairy dust into the envelope, and seal it with wax from both the candles.
- Extinguish the candles.
- Close the circle.
- Leave the envelope on your altar for the night in between the two candles.
- The next day, bury the envelopes and candles outside.

Passion Candles

Cast this spell during the Waxing Moon to attract romantic passion into your life.

Supplies:
> Red candle wax
> Pink candle wax
> Candle Molds (open glass jars or something similar)
> Candle wicks
> Jasmine oil
> Dried apple blossoms
> Mortar and pestle
> Double Boiler

Instructions:
- Set a safe space intention for your kitchen.
- In a double boiler, melt the red candle wax.
- While making the candles, visualize your intention for romantic passion. Hold that image while you make the candles.
- As the wax melts, set up wicks in your candle molds.
- You'll be making an equal number of pink and red candles to plan molds accordingly.
- Add 10-15 drops of jasmine oil to the melted wax.
- Use the mortar and pestle to grind up the apple blossoms.
- Add half of the blossom powder to the red melted wax and mix well.
- Remove wax from the heat and pour into half of the molds.
- Return the double boiler to the stove, and put the pink candle wax in.
- Once it is melted, add 10-15 drops of jasmine oil and the remaining apple blossom powder. Mix together.
- Remove from the heat and pour into the remaining molds.
- Allow the wax to cool and solidify.
- Burn a red and pink candle together every night, following the spell until you have used them all up.

Strengthen Love

Cast this spell on a Full Moon or New Moon to strengthen an existing romantic relationship. Have permission from your partner before casting the spell. It's primarily designed to overcome hurdles in a relationship or repair damage in a relationship.

Supplies:
- White candle
- Blue candle
- Pink candle
- Picture of you and your partner together

Instructions:
- Before casting this spell, get the expressed consent from your partner.
- Open your Sacred Circle.
- Cleanse the three candles.
- Set your candles on the altar in a triangle shape, and set the image of you and your partner at the center of the triangle.
- Light the white candle and say:
  - *A white light to cleanse and heal*
- Light the blue candle and say:
  - *A blue light for forgiveness and removing obstacles*
- Light the pink candle and say:
  - *A pink light to restore love and affection*
- Pour three drops of candle wax from each of the candles on the picture.
- Say this incantation three times:
  To the Goddess and God, I make this plea
  Rekindle this passion times three
  Please restore this love anew
  By white, pink, and blue
  With these words, this spell is done
  Work my will, and harm none
- Take some time to meditate on the burning candles. Visualize what you want your relationship to turn into. Focus on the good times, happiness, balance, and good communication. Think of specific experiences that you've had where you want to feel that way again with your partner.
- Close the circle.
- Extinguish the candles, and bury the candle stubs and picture outside.

Love can be felt and expressed in many ways. Although most of the spells in this section are geared toward romantic love, there are spells for a familial friend and self-love that you are encouraged to explore.

Giving thanks for love is another way to cast love spells. These chapters are just a preliminary guide to what you can do with magic and what kinds of spells you can cast. This just scratches the surface of the world of magic for you to explore!

As you learn more about Wicca, magic, and spells, you will begin to see how love is such an important part of the Wiccan lifestyle and religion.

It cannot be said enough that magic and spells are not to be used for manipulation or control. Whenever you look to cast a spell for love, the intent is to have an open mind about drawing a lover or relationship to you that is right for you and the other person.

You can never know what really is in another person's heart. Rather than trying to control their actions and affections, trust the universe and trust the Goddess and God to bring you the love and relationship you need and deserve. Not only will they guide you to the love that is right for you, but they will also guide the right lover to you.

Chapter Seven: Spells for Wellness

What does wellness mean? Generally speaking, wellness refers to well-being and even health. If you are healthy in body, mind, and emotional state, then you have achieved wellness.

Unfortunately, being healthy and well isn't always that easy. There are a lot of factors to consider, such as diet, exercise, and lifestyle, as well as genetics.

Any time someone engages in negative habits or lifestyle choices, it creates an energy imbalance in the body. This imbalance leads to illness, sickness, and even injury. This can be physical, mental, and emotional.

Since magic works with energy and balance, you can use spells to heal and restore wellness. That makes sense, doesn't it!? Of course, it does.

This section of the book is going to focus on healing spells. Some are wide-ranged, and others are focused on a specific ailment. Healing doesn't just have to be for an ailment or injury, though. It can be about personal wellness, such as beauty and emotions. It can also be about clearing negative and unwanted energies out of your living space.

Going back to the law 'An Harm None, Do what you Will,' it can be hard to watch a family member, friend, or loved one struggle with illness, disease, or injury. The thought of casting a spell to help them is very appealing. Spells can be helpful, but even in this scenario, it is still important to get the permission of someone before casting a spell on them, even if the intention is as pure as healing them.

The universe doesn't always give us a clear path to follow. It may not seem like it, but there are reasons for what goes on. If someone you know is sick and agrees to allow you to heal them with a spell, then that is absolutely fine. Some Wiccans provide healing spells as a paid service!

Remember that healing can be offered in many forms. There doesn't always have to be magic involved. Sometimes, a simple touch or just being there is enough to heal someone's pain.

Heal Your Past
Cast this spell during the Waxing Moon to heal past traumas.

Supplies:
  1 cup Epsom salts
  ½ cup baking soda
  Pine oil
  Lavender oil
  Blue food dye (crushed blueberries for a natural color)

Instructions:
- Set a safety intention for your bathroom.
- Mix the Epsom salts and baking soda together.
- Add five drops each of the lavender oil and pine oils.
- Mix in the blueberries to give the bath salts a blue hue.
- Sprinkle the bath salts into the tub, and draw a warm bath.
- Let the salts dissolve in the water and then soak in the bath.
- As you soak, think about past traumas you experienced, and let the salts soak your past away. Visualize the water actually dissolving your past as it dissolves the bath salts.
- If any emotions arise while you soak, let yourself feel them; don't hold back.
- Let go of any harmful thoughts and negative memories.
- Repeat this bath as frequently as you would like.

Banish Depression

This spell is best cast during the Waning Moon.

Supplies:
> Clear glass cup of spring or rain water
> Mud
> Black candle

Instructions:
- Cast your Sacred Circle.
- Bless the black candle.
- Light the black candle.
- Hold the mud in your left hand, and focus your depression on it. Focus all negative thoughts and feelings you have into that mud.
- Say this incantation three times:
  > *Depression, I banish you*
  > *Leave my body, mind, and soul too!*
- Put the mud into the water, and blow out the black candle.
- Close your circle.
- Set the glass in a bright window, and allow for the water to start dissolving the mud. As the mud dissolves, so will your depression.
- After 2-3 weeks, return the mud to the earth and dispel the rest of your depression with it.

Banish Negative Energy

This spell is best cast during the Waxing Moon. It's a spell designed to banish negative energies from a specific room or space.

> Supplies:
>> Sage smudge stick
>> Pine needles
>> Smudging feather
>> Rose water

Instructions:
- Set a sacred and safe space intention for the room you are banishing negative energy from.
- Light your sage smudge bundle, and use the smudging feathers to waft the smoke around the room, focusing on the corners.
- As you smudge, repeat this chant:
  > *Negative energies I cast you out*
  > *I purify this space with a shout*
  > *I protect this space from unwanted forces*
  > *I banish you all at your sources*
- Anoint the windows and doors of that room with rose water.
- Hang small bundles of pine needles in each window.

Spell for Inner Peace

Cast this spell on the Full Moon.

Supplies:
    White candle
    Lavender oil
    Calm music
    Pen
    Book of Shadows or Grimoire

Instructions:
- Cast the Sacred Circle.
- Cleanse your white candle.
- Set the calming music on a low volume, and light the candle. Anoint your temples, third eyes, and heart chakra (forehead and center of chest) with the lavender oil.
- Meditate on the intended goal of reaching a state of inner peace.
- Once you feel yourself in a calm and relaxed state, take out your Grimoire or Book of Shadows and begin to write down your feeling and thoughts.
- Continue to meditate until you feel serene and like you have nothing left to write
- Blow the white candle out.
- Close your circle.

Heal Apathy

Cast this spell during the Waning Moon to reconnect with your body and feelings.

> Supplies:
> > Green candle
> > Blank paper and pen
> > Green cloth, made of natural fibers
> > Rose petals
> > Thyme
> > String

Instructions:
- Open the Sacred Circle.
- Cleanse the green candle.
- Light your candle.
- On the blank sheet of paper, write out a list of feelings, and speak each one aloud. Write memories in which you remember having strong emotions, preferably positive emotions.
- Repeat the list of emotions again.
- Fold the paper three times and set it in the center of the green cloth.
- Sprinkle rose petals and thyme over the paper.
- Tie the cloth up into a sachet, and keep it under your pillow.
- Close the circle.
- Over the next several days, reach out to people physically, and start reorienting yourself through physical touch.
- When you begin to feel a full range of emotions again, bury the sachet outside.

Healing Meditation

Perform this healing spell during the Waxing Moon. If you are performing this healing meditation on someone else, get their prior consent before performing the spell.

Supplies:
Sage smudge bundle
White candle

Instructions:
- If necessary, get the consent of the person you are performing this spell for
- Cast the Sacred Circle.
- Cleanse the white candle.
- Light the candle and the sage bundle.
- Let the sage smolder in a heatproof dish. Cup the smoke in your hands, and wash it over your body.
- Let your mind sink into a deeper meditative state.
- Breathe deeply, connecting to your inner spirits. If you know your spirit guides, connect with them as well.
- Keep meditating, and open your mind to spiritual healing. Focus on finding your healing path.
- Imagine what you or the person you are performing the spell for looks like in their full health. View them or yourself after the healing has happened.
- Imagine yourself or them healthy in a week, a month from now, one year, or five years.
- Keep meditating until the sage bundle and the candle burns out.
- Close the circle.
- Take the sage ashes and the candle stub outside to bury.

Healing Tree Spell

Cast this spell during the Waxing Moon or Full Moon. This spell is to heal a wounded tree back to health. You should ask the tree for a sign that it is open to receive healing.

Supplies:
White candle
Red towel
Bowl or rain or spring water

Instructions:
- Get permission from the tree to perform a healing spell.
- Stand in front of the tree that you are healing. Set a safety intention for the space around the tree.
- Cleanse the candle.
- Stick the candle in the ground and light it (if there are any fire hazards nearby, clear the surrounding area before lighting the candle).
- Pour the bowl of water around the roots of the tree, walking deosil (clockwise) around the trunk.
- Lay the red towel down around the trunk of the tree, and visualize what the tree will look like when it is healed and healthy again.
- Place your hands on the tree and say this incantation three times:
  Tree spirit, mighty and strong
  You sing to me a sad song
  My magic works a healing charm
  This is my will, doing no harm
- Blow the candle out; do not let it burn down as that is a potential fire hazard.
- Send positive energy and vibes toward the tree when it crosses your mind.

Healing Brew

Cast this spell during the Waxing Moon.

Supplies:
> 1 tablespoon ground willow bark
> 1 teaspoon vanilla extract
> Pinch of rosemary
> 3-6 dried apple slices
> Sugar
> Boiling water
> Tea cup or mug
> Plate

Instructions:
- Set a safe and sacred intention space in your kitchen.
- While making the brew, visualize your goal and intention, infusing them with healing energy.
- In the bottom of a mug or teacup, put the willow bark, vanilla extract, rosemary, and apple slices.
- Boil 2-3 cups of water on the stove in a saucepan or a teapot.
- Pour the boiling water into the mug over the healing ingredients.
- Cover the mug with the plate, and allow the brew to steep for 3-5 minutes.
- Uncover and taste the brew; add sugar to sweeten it as desired.
- Once cool enough to drink, drink the entire cup.
- Use this brew once or twice a week for treating an ongoing ailment.

Healthy Skin Spell
Cast this spell on the Full Moon for the most potent effects.

Supplies:
> Rose petals, dried
> Lavender Flowers, dried
> Rosemary, dried
> Washcloth
> Rubber band
> Boiling water

Instructions:
- Set a safe, sacred intention for your kitchen.
- In the washcloth, combine the dried herbs and then bind them in a bundle with the rubber band.
- Boil water on the stove. Once it reaches boiling point, turn the heat off, and set the washcloth bundle into the water, submerging it completely.
- Visualize healthy, clear skin, and keep that image as you work this spell.
- While the herbs are steeping, repeat this incantation three times:
> *Healthy beauty is my wish*
> *Clear my skin from any blemish*
> *Goddess grant me beautiful skin*
> *Now forever, always been*
- Once the water is cool enough to touch, take the washcloth out and give it a gentle squeeze.
- Use the herb washcloth to spread the water on your face, neck, chest, arms, and the rest of your body. Continue to bathe yourself this way until all the water in the pot has been used on your skin.

Sleep Well Spell

Cast this spell during the Waning Moon to banish nightmares.

Supplies:
Fabric, made of a natural fiber
Dried chamomile
Dried rosemary
String
Light blue candle

Instructions:
- Cast a Sacred Circle.
- Cleanse the blue candle.
- Light the candle on your altar.
- Set out the fabric and combine equal parts of the dried herbs in the center of the fabric.
- Drip three drops of light blue candle wax into the combined herbs.
- Tie up your bag with the string. As you tie it, say this incantation three times:
    To prevent nightmares
    I cast this spell
    To wake every morn
    Refreshed and well
- Close the circle.

- Sleep with the charm bag under your pillow to banish nightmares.

Heal by Moonlight
Cast this spell on the Full Moon for healing.

Supplies:
> White candle

Instructions:
- Cast your Sacred Circle.
- Cleanse the white candle.
- Set the candle on your altar and light it. Stare into the flame of the candle, meditating on the flame. Envision yourself healing or being healed. Focus on your healing intention and continue to meditate.
- When you are called to, say this incantation three times:
  > *By the healing power of Moon and Starlight*
  > *Silver Goddess, lend me your might*
  > *Heal me inside, heal me outside*
  > *I implore you, please, be my guide*
  > *This spell is my will*
  > *So mote it be*
- Again, meditate on the candle flame and your healing intention. Meditate until the candle burns out.
- Close the circle.
- Bury the candle stub outside under the light of the Full Moon.

Relieve Anxiety

Cast this spell on the Waning Moon or New Moon.

Supplies:
- Cauldron
- Black candle
- Amethyst crystal
- Jade crystal
- Onyx Crystal
- Chamomile
- Thyme
- Rosemary
- Lavender
- Mortar and pestle
- Hot water
- Glass jar

Instructions:
- Cast a Sacred Circle.
- Cleanse the black candle.
- Light the candle on your altar.
- Use the mortar and pestle to mash up the fresh herbs and then put them in your cauldron.
- As you are grinding the herbs, say:
  With these herbs, I invoke calm, peace, harmony, and serenity
- Envision yourself being internally and externally calm and peaceful.
- Add the three stones to the cauldron and say:
  Amethyst, Onyx, and Jade to relax and soothe body and soul
- Pour the warm water over the herbs and crystals.
- Place your hands on either side of the cauldron and say:
  Goddess and God, please grant me peace
  Set my mind and soul at ease
  Release me from this anxiety
  This is my will, so mote it be
- Pick up the candle and drip wax from the black candle into the mixture.
- Anoint your temples, third eye chakra, and heart chakra (forehead and center of the chest) with the potion.
- Sink into a relaxing meditation until the candle burns out.
- Say:
  Anxiety, I banish thee!

- Close the circle.
- Keep a portion of the potion in a glass jar and pour the rest outside. Anoint yourself with a few drops of the potion any time you are feeling anxious.

Burn Healing Lotion
Cast this spell during a Waxing Moon.

Supplies:
- Coconut oil
- Dried rosemary
- Filtered water or spring water
- Cheesecloth
- Glass container

Instructions:
- Set a safe and sacred intention in your kitchen.
- While making this burn lotion, continue to focus on its healing properties so that the lotion gets infused with that intention.
- On the stovetop, boil the water with a few pinches of rosemary.
- Let the herb boil for 3-5 minutes.
- Turn the heat off, and use cheesecloth to strain out the rosemary.
- While the water is still warm, stir in 3-5 tablespoons of coconut oil.
- Blend together well; transfer the mixture into a bowl, and put it in the refrigerator.
- Once the mix has cooled for about 30 minutes, skim off the coconut butter.
- Discard the water, and transfer the butter lotion into a glass container.
- This can be used directly on fresh burns.
- Use this lotion on new and old scars to help heal the scar tissue.
- Store in a cool, dark place.

Animal Healing Spell

Cast this spell during the Waxing or Full Moon. You can cast on the animal directly or on an image of the animal from a distance. Ask for some indication that the animal gives you permission to perform the healing spell.

Supplies:
> 2 brown candles
> 5 quartz crystals
> Blank paper and pen
> Image of animal (if being cast from a distance)

Instructions:
- Ask for some kind of indication of permission from the animal before you cast this spell.
- Cast your sacred circle.
- Cleanse the brown candles.
- Visualize the animal regaining health and wellness as you perform the next two steps.
- Set the crystals in a circle around the animal or the image of the animal
- Light the two candles.
- Hover your hands over the animal or over their picture.
- Repeat this incantation three times:
  > *Hunter God, I ask of you, to restore the balance here within*
  > *Restore this animal's life and health again*
  > *Health in body, spirit, and mind*
  > *Grant us this favor in kind*
  > *Harm none is a must*
  > *My words cast this spell, in you I trust*
- Focus on your goal and intention as you chant.
- Blow out the candles.
- Close the circle.
- Repeat this spell for three consecutive nights.
- When you are done, bury the candle stubs in the ground.

Simple Healing Spell

Cast this spell during the Waxing Moon. It can be used to heal yourself or someone else. If you are healing someone else, get their permission before casting the spell.

Supplies:
5 white candles

Instructions:
- Open the Sacred circle.
- Cleanse your five candles.
- Sit cross-legged at your altar.
- Set Four of the candles around where you are sitting, one each at the four cardinal directions, north, south, east, and west
- Set the fifth candle right in front of you.
- Light the candles, and begin to meditate. Focus on the goal of healing yourself or the person you are casting the spell for.
- Once you have entered a meditative state, repeat this incantation three times:
  Health, wellness, and good fortune I seek
  To the Mother Goddess and Father God, I speak
  Surround me with a healing light
  This is my wish for this rite
- Lapse back into a meditative state while focusing the healing intention on yourself or the person you are casting the spell for.
- Blow the candles out.
- Close the circle.
- Repeat this spell for nine consecutive nights.
- Bury the candle stubs when done.

Chakra Healing Charm

Cast this spell during the Waxing Moon or at the Full Moon. It is designed to balance, open, and heal energetic chakras.

Supplies:
Leather drawstring pouch
White string
Dried Marjoram
Dried Sage
Dried Chamomile
Dried Angelica
Dried Jasmine
Dried Mugwort
Dried Basil
Dried Lilac
Dried Lavender
Mortar and Pestle
Cauldron

Instructions:
- Cast your Sacred Circle.
- Use the mortar and pestle to crush each dried herb individually.
- Once an herb has been powdered, pour it into the cauldron and start grinding the next herb.
- As you are grinding the herbs, visualize the goal of your spell. Envision each of the seven major chakras opening up and energy flowing smoothly between them.
- Once all the herbs are powered and in the cauldron, mix them together to form a blended powder.
- Place your hands on either side of the cauldron.
- Repeat this incantation three times:
  Root, sacral, solar plexus too
  These herbs I blend to heal you
  Heart, throat, and third eye
  Balance energy and detoxify
  Crown chakra in the mix as well
  The words I speak cast this spell
- While you chant, continue to envision the chakras existing in a healthy, energetic state.
- Pour the chakra powder into the leather drawstring pouch.
- Close the circle.

- Wear the pouch around your neck or on your person for three days and nights.
- After that, wear the pouch whenever you feel that your energy is unbalanced

Keeping yourself healthy should be a top priority. Sometimes, society can make us think that taking care of ourselves is selfish. Don't listen to that! Self-improvement and self-healing are constant. If you don't look after your own wellness, no one else will.

Generally speaking, Wiccans seek to help others and heal the world around them. This is also important. However, you can't offer strength and healing to anyone or anything else if you haven't worked on yourself first.

Any time you perform a healing spell, you can encounter strong feelings and emotional responses. During spells, if emotions arise, do not try to hold them back. Let them flow freely. This can help the healing because unexpressed and bottled emotions create imbalances and disease within the body.

Although healing yourself is important, wellness doesn't just extend to personal health. It can relate to energetic states in a specific space or a person; it can be about improving your sleep and reducing stress and anxiety. As you continue to work with magic and spells, you'll start to intuitively find times when you can improve your own wellness with spells or small prayers and incantations.

Allow yourself the kindness of working on your own wellness and then extend that to people, animals, and other things that give you permission to do so.

Chapter Eight: Other Tools and Strategies

By now, you should have a solid understanding of Wicca, magic, and spells. Maybe you have even tried a few of the spells in the previous chapters! You should be at a good point to keep journeying on your Wiccan Path. Now, it is time to take a slightly deeper look into some of the topics that have only been touched on in earlier chapters.

Topics to be covered in this chapter include:

- Wiccan Holidays, Sabbats, and Esbats
- Moon Cycles
- Elements
- Uncommon Wiccan Tools

The information in this book is designed to be a starting point, so if you come across a topic that you want to learn more about, you are definitely encouraged to do so.

Esbats

Esbats are celebratory rituals that celebrate the Moon and the moon phases. Goddess energy is strongly associated with the moon, so these rituals often have a focus on honoring the Goddess and her energy. Many Covens like to gather on both the Full Moon and New Moon for rituals, but the moon can be celebrated and worked with during any of its phases.

Every year, there are 12 to 13 Full Moons. The moon energy tends to be at its strongest when the moon is full. However, the energy changes as the moon moves through its cycles. The main phases of the moon are the Full Moon, Waning Moon, New Moon, and Waxing Moon. As a Wiccan, you can hold Esbats at any time of the moon cycle and even hold more than once a month, especially if you are a Solitary Practitioner.

New Moon
A New Moon is when the moon does not appear in the sky. New Moon energy is great for new beginnings. Now is the time to start new projects or plan or take a new adventure. Under the power of the New Moon, build a new life, a new career, a new love, and a new you!

Waxing Moon

The Waxing Moon is the period of the moon cycle when the moon is growing from new to full. Every night, it gets a little larger in the sky. The energy of the Waxing Moon is about growth. With the energy of the Waxing Moon, keep working on what you have already started to build. This could be a career, a relationship, or financial success. As the moon grows, you will start to feel the Goddesses energy more strongly.

Full Moon

This is when the moon is complete in the sky and at the peak of its power. The Goddess energy of the Full Moon is when you should work to get what you want. At the Full Moon, you can work to accomplish just about anything. Full Moon energy is great for the magic that has to do with divination, love, dreams, and goals. The Full Moon energy can be accessed up to three nights before and three nights after the actual full moon. You may have already felt Full Moon energy without the use of magic; many people do, and that is how strong it is!

Waning Moon

During the Waning Moon, the moon is decreasing in size, going from full to new. Every night, the moon appears smaller in the sky. The Waning Moon is the best time for banishing magic. It is the time to get rid of anything negative or that no longer serves your highest good. Cast some extra weight, illness, or negative thoughts away.

Each Full Moon also has special properties and associations, depending on when in the year the moon occurs.

Wolf Moon

This is the January Full Moon, associated with protection and strength. This moon is both a time of beginning and end. It is also known as the Cold or Winter Moon.

Storm Moon

The February moon. This is a time of fertility, magic and strength. In preindustrial days, this was the hardest time of the year. It is also known as the Death or Quickening Moon.

Chaste Moon

This is the March Full Moon. Now is the time to plant mental seeds, change thought patterns, and foster thoughts of success and hope. There are also associations of purity and newness. It is time to prepare yourself mentally for new experiences. It is also called the Worm Moon.

Seed Moon

The Full Moon of April. Now is the time to sow magical seeds. If you are planting a garden, especially one of herbs and magical plants, now is the time to start (this is going to depend on the geographical region you live in). You can also put plants in pots and start growing them indoors. It is time to stop planning and start enacting your plans. It is also referred to as the Egg, Grass, or Wind Moon.

Hare Moon

This is the May Full Moon. The Hare Moon is the time of love, health, wisdom, and romance. Now is a good time to rekindle the passion in romantic relationships. It is also referred to as the Flower or Planting Moon.

Lover's Moon

June brings us the Lover's Moon. Here, we get energy for love, success, and marriage. It is also called the Strawberry or Rose Moon.

Mead Moon

In July, we have the Mead Moon. This is a true time of enchantment. It is associated with health, rebirth, success, and strength—a great time of celebration and magic. Prosperity magic is potent at this time. It is also known as the Lightening, Blessing, or Thunder Moon.

Wyrt Moon

In August, we have the Wyrt Moon. Energies are associated with abundance, marriage, and agriculture. It is also called the Wort, Corn, or Red Moon.

Harvest Moon

This moon belongs to September. Energies for protection and prosperity are strong. Abundance, especially magic to provide abundance to others (with their permission), is potent.

Blood Moon

The Full Moon of October. This moon is representative of new goals, resolution, protection, and spirituality. Divination is strong at this time. It is also a time of reflecting on your accomplishments through the past year. It is also referred to as the Hunter or Falling Leaf Moon.

Snow Moon

This is November's Full Moon. Familial bonds and friendship bonds are strong, and the energies are right to work with them. It is also a time of prosperity and abundance. Divination for future situations is potent at this time. Winter is approaching, but remember that it will not last forever. Also, it is known as the Beaver, Tree, or Mourning Moon.

Oak Moon

December brings us the Oak Moon. Now is a time of hope and healing. This is the time of the year when the moon reigns because it has more hours in a day than the sun. It is time to let go of old patterns and break habits. Turn to the rebirth of light with the Winter Solstice, and look to rebirth and renew.

Esbats can be performed for any phase of the moon, for any of the Full Moons. You can find prewritten rituals in books and online. However, when you make your own rituals, they tend to align much better with your personal energies, and it becomes a better way to honor spirit, deity, and yourself.

Sabbats

The term Sabbat refers to the eight different Wiccan holidays that occur throughout the year. These holidays represent the turning of the Wheel of the Year, a concept that celebrates how the seasons change and what each change means for the earth's energy, life, and Goddess and God energy.

The Wheel of the Year is a concept that with every rotation the earth completes, it begins another one. The seasons cycle every rotation, and this means that there are changes in lifestyle based on the seasons. Winter months have very different energy and connotation than the summer months.

The Sabbats are naturally occurring times during the year. While the modern Wiccan calendar has designated specific days for these holidays, in ancient times, the celebration occurred at the relevant time of year. Sometimes, the celebration lasted weeks or even a month, depending on the type of celebration.

While Sabbats can be celebrated with a prewritten or standardized ritual, it is important to observe them for the entire day, not just the designated ritual time. There are tasks and actions for each Sabbat that can help you honor the rite throughout the day.

Samhain

Pronounced *Sow-inn*, Samhain occurs on October 31st on the modern calendar. This is the Wiccan New Year. Samhain is a time of endings and new beginnings. It is also the last of the three harvest Sabbats. The veil between the spirit worlds and our world is thinnest. Since the veil is thinnest, honoring ancestors and deceased loved ones is a strong theme at this time. Divination is also at its strongest for Samhain. Samhain is one of the fire rituals as well, often celebrated with great bonfires. The Sun God dies at Samhain, meaning that darker days are upon the world. Jack-o-lanterns, as well as masks and costumes, have been used for centuries to ward off evil spirits. These traditions have been adapted into Halloween celebrations.

Yule

The Winter Solstice or Yule occurs on December 21st, give or take a few days. The Sun God is reborn. Many of the Christmas traditions, such as wreaths, decorated trees, wassail, and festival lights were taken from Wiccan traditions and adapted to Christian beliefs. Some Wiccans find this distasteful; however, focusing on your own beliefs and celebrations is what is important.

Light begins to return to the earth now that the God has been reborn. While he is still growing and gaining strength, Yule is a time of hope and looking to a brighter future. Rituals that involve candles are common as a representation of the returning sun. The Sun God will grow and then become the lover of the Goddess and father to the next incarnation of the Sun God.

Imbolc

Imbolc occurs on February 2nd. The God is a child, and the Goddess recovers from giving birth. Imbolc is a time to celebrate the Goddess as she turns the Wheel of the Year toward spring again. Winter was harsh in ancient times; many people succumbed to starvation, illness, and the cold, resulting in death. Using ritual to call spring and the return of warmth and life was an effort to stave off such hardships. Even if the land is still covered with snow or ice, Imbolc is a time to prepare for the coming spring and season of planting. Strewing salt and herbs across the earth is a ritual action to help get the earth ready for the planting season.

Ostara

Ostara is the Vernal Equinox or Spring Equinox. It occurs on March 21st, give or take a few days. Easter has adapted many of the symbols associated with Ostara, such as colored eggs and candy as gifts. For Ostara, it uses eggs as symbolism for fertility and new growth. The Maiden Goddess is becoming a woman and entering her fertile years.

The earth is becoming fertile, and animals and livestock are beginning to produce offspring.

The day and night are equal. The Goddess and God are seen as innocent children. Blessing seeds for planting, having egg hunts, and eating chocolate bunnies are common Ostara rituals.

Beltane

May 1st is when Beltane occurs. It is the celebration of the union of the Goddess and God in their marriage. The God is now the lord of animals, and the Goddess is the queen of faeries and flowers. From Beltane to Samhain, the sun reigns strongly. Raising a maypole to dance around is a common celebration of Beltane. Fertility is a strong theme as this is when the Goddess and God marry and conceive the next incarnation of the God.

Flower crowns and garlands are exchanged and worn. Bonfires are lit in celebration. Dancing around bonfires under the night sky is a traditional practice. Joining in the flesh in a sexual ritual is also a Beltane ritual, another fire ritual.

Litha

The Summer Solstice is also Litha, happening on June 21st, give or take a few days. Nature has reached its peak. The Goddess and God are at the height of their powers, and the veil between worlds is thin again. This is the longest day of the year and a time to celebrate vitality, creativity, health, vigor, and abundance. Blessings for animals are performed at this time of year.

Herbs for magic and medicinal uses have reached their potency point, and it is time to gather and dry them for use. Stone circles have been used in Litha celebrations for thousands of years. Many are still standing all across Europe. It is a time of wish-granting and fulfillment.

Lughnasad

Lughnasad is the first harvest ritual, occurring on August 1st or 2nd. The first harvest often includes grains and starchy plants such as wheat and corn. Some vegetables are also ready to be harvested now too.

Actions and tasks that symbolize the harvest include parts of the harvested plants that aren't being consumed or stored. Both Goddess and God energies are still strong, and celebrations of abundance are at their highest. It is the time to honor the Goddess and

God for their fertility and the bountiful harvests produced to last through the winters. It is a great time of celebration but also a reminder that winter is approaching and harder times are ahead.

Mabon

Mabon is the second harvest festival. It occurs on September 21st, give or take a few days. It is the Autumnal equinox when the day and night are again equal, after which the days grow shorter, leading to the death of the God. This harvest is for fruits and some of the later vegetables. The God prepares for his death, and the Goddess begins to mourn her loss. Cornucopias, corn husk wreaths, and grand harvest feasts are held at this time. Wine is usually ready for consumption and done so in great quantities for celebration.

Each of the eight Sabbats is equally as important. You can use prewritten rituals, write your own, or just make one up at the time of the celebration. If you are in a Coven, the Coven most likely has reconstructed rituals for their Sabbat celebrations.

Each Sabbat holds great significance and honors the Goddess and God in different ways, as well as the seasons and the running year.

Elements

In Wicca, there are four basic elements that make up the source of magic. Every single energetic force, including humans, has elemental associations to at least one of these four elements.

The elements are earth, air, water, and fire. As you continue to study Wicca, you will see these elements come up again and again. You can work magic directly with any of these elements, or you can combine them with other magic.

Earth

The element of earth represents strength, abundance, wealth, stability, and femininity. Earth magic can be used in the form of herbs or the use of salt, sand, or dirt on the altar. Earth magic can take the form of gardening, crystal and stonework, knot magic, binding spells, grounding, runes, and money and treasure.

Earth is feminine in nature and associated with the direction North. Symbols include rocks, salt, fields, soil, and clay.

Goddesses associated with the element earth are Demeter, Ceres, Persephone, Rhea, Gaia, Nephtys, and Mah.

Earth Gods include Athos, Adonis, Tammuz, Pan, Cernunnos, Dionysus, Arwan, and Mardyk.

Gnomes, dwarves, and trolls are the kind of spiritual creatures associated with earth.

The season for the earth is winter. Zodiac signs associated with earth are Taurus, Virgo, and Capricorn. Colors include brown, green, yellow, and black.

Air

The element of air represents the mind. It is associated with intelligence, telepathy, communication, imagination, ideas, inspiration, dreams, knowledge, and wishes. When used in ritual, air can be symbolized by an object being tossed into the air. Aromatherapy, songs, burning incense, playing the flute, and hanging objects in trees. Divination is associated with air, as is wind magic, prophecy, and karmic work.

Air is a masculine element that is associated with the direction east. Symbols of air include wind, breezes, the sky, feathers, clouds, breath, smoke, trees, and vibrations.

Goddesses associated with air include Nuit, Urania, Aradia, Cardea, and Arianhod.

Gods associated with the element air are Thoth, Shu, Enlil, Kheohevo, and Merawrim.

The spirits of the Air include faeries or fairies, sylphs, and zephyrs.

Spring is the season for air. Colors include yellow, white, and crimson. The zodiac associations with the element air are Libra, Gemini, and Aquarius.

Water

The element of water represents emotions, with associations of the subconscious mind, absorption, eternal movement, purification, wisdom, the soul, and emotional aspects of love. In rituals, water can be represented by pouring water over objects, making brews, or tossing objects into the water. Bathing, cold herbal infusions, and sprinkling water are all ritual actions for water, as well. Mirror divination, magnet magic, lucid dreaming, love magic, protection, and cleansing magic are associated with water.

Water is a feminine element that corresponds to the direction west. Symbols of water include the ocean, streams, rivers, rain, lakes, shells, springs, frogs, wells, fog, and chalices, cups, or goblets.

Water goddesses include Isis, Aphrodite, Mari, Marianne, Yemaha, and Tiamat.

Gods that are associated with water include Ea, Dylan, Osiris, Neptune, Poseidon, and Manannan.

Nymphs, udines, and mermaids are spirit creatures that are associated with water.

The season associated with water is autumn or fall. Colors of water include blue, turquoise, grey, indigo, green, and black. The zodiac signs that relate to water are Cancer, Scorpio, and Pisces.

Fire

Fire is a wild element. It is associated with energy, love, inspiration, and leadership. In rituals, fire is represented as burning objects, baking or cooking, and lighting candles. It is an element of change. Cauldron magic is also associated with fire. Types of magic include candle spells, healing, love magic, and energy work.

Fire is a masculine element, the most spiritual, physical, and magical of the elements. Fire is representative of the direction south. It is symbolized by flames, lightning, volcanoes, heated objects, sun, stars, lava, heat, and rainbows.

Goddesses associated with the element fire include Pele, Brigit, Vesta, and Hestia.

Fire gods include Horus, Vulcan, Prometheus, and Agni.

Spirits of fire include salamanders, drakes, and dragons.

Fire is associated with the summer season. The colors that represent fire include gold, red, crimson, orange, and white. The zodiac signs that are associated with fire are Aries, Leo, and Sagittarius.

As a general precaution, when working with fire, it is best to work in an open space in a heatproof cauldron, fireplace, wood stove, or a designated fire pit. It is not a bad idea to have water on hand in case the fire gets a little feisty.

Spirit, Ether, or Aether is commonly considered a fifth element. While it is included in elemental charts as the element that gives life and it can be used magic, it isn't one of the four base elements.

Spirit

Spirit is the primary element in all things. It is associated with space, connection, balance, and harmony. Spirit is needed for the other four elements to exist. Spirit is an immaterial element; it doesn't have a physical form or representation. It represents a feeling of joy, connectedness, and union.

The Goddess and God associations for Spirit are the Horned God and the Lady Goddess. It is represented in the seasons as the complete Wheel of the Year. The color that represents Spirit is White.

If you have representations on your altar for the four elements, you can also include the Spirit if you so wish.

Working with the elements can be truly powerful. Elemental magic can change weather patterns, enhance spells and rituals, and be used for an innumerable number of spells and rituals. You may not even realize how much you already integrate the elements into your spells and daily life.

Elements have personality associations to individuals as well. Knowing what elements that you correspond with your personality traits can also help your magic. Finding an aligned element to include in spells and rituals will further enhance your magical potency.

Uncommon Wiccan Tools

In the first chapter, we covered some of the basic tools used in Wicca that are commonly found on the altar. In Wicca, there are some tools that are specific to traditions or types of magic that are also worth mentioning.

You may find that you want to include these optional or less common tools in your practice, especially if they correspond to your tradition or preferred magic type. When referring to the tools as 'uncommon' or 'less common,' that just means they aren't part of the 'basic' altar setup. Many Wiccans still use them.

Some of the less common tools that will be discussed in this chapter include:

- Boline
- Bell
- Libation Dish
- Deity
- Pentacle
- Smudge Feathers
- Crystals

- Staff
- Sword

You may find a resonation with some of these tools and decide to incorporate them in your practice.

Boline

The Boline is a traditional herb knife. It is a white-handled, bone-handled, or sickle-shaped blade. One edge is often serrated while the other is smooth.

The Boline is a knife that is most commonly used in herb magic. Whether it is for harvesting plant and herb material outside or cutting and preparing herbs in the kitchen or on the altar, the Boline is the tool for the job!

Bell

Bells can be set on the altar and used when casting circles, closing circles, and raising energy during spells and rituals. A strong tone can help induce a meditative state. Bells are considered to be the voice of the Goddess. Ringing a bell can call the divine to you. The sound of bells can also change the vibration of energy in and around you, enhancing positivity.

Bells come in all shapes, sizes, and tones. If you'd like to use a bell, make sure to find a tone that resonates with you. Keep it on your altar or near your altar.

Libation Dish

When honoring the Goddess, God, Spirits, and other Deities, setting out offerings to them is a way of showing gratitude and faith. Some Wiccans prefer having a designated libation dish for their offerings.

This dish can be a regular bowl, an open shell, or any kind of receptacle with a personal value that can hold an offering.

Deity

Since Wicca is a religion, there is a lot of work done with the Goddess and God. Since there is a common belief that all gods are one god and all goddesses are one Goddess, and we all resonate with deity differently, you may find a connection to a specific deity.

There are a countless number of deities from Celtic, Nordic, Roman, Greek, Egyptian, and dozens of other traditions around the world. Many of them have names and associations that can come up in Wiccan practices.

If you find a resonation with a deity that you want to use in spells and pay homage to, then it might be a good idea to have a representation of them on your altar. A picture, figurine, or natural object that is associated with them can work.

Pentacle

Pentacles or Pentagrams, unfortunately, have a negative association with Satanism. There is some speculation to suggest that it was a Christian ploy to deter popularity in Wiccan traditions.

The pentacle is a five-pointed star in a circle. The points of the star represent each of the four elements, as well as the spirit. Having a strong association with the earth, the pentacle is a great tool to combine the elements in magic.

You can make your own, draw one, set candles out in a pentacle, or wear one around your neck. Integrating pentacles into your work isn't necessary, but some Wiccans resonate with that symbol.

Smudge Feathers

Smudge feathers are used to waft incense smoke, and smoke from smudge sticks are wafted around a space. It can be a single feather or a feather bundle.

If you find yourself doing a lot of smudging or air work, then smudge feathers might be a tool you find yourself interested in.

Crystals

Crystals come in so many shapes, colors, and sizes. Their energy is potent and powerful because of their unique, crystalline, geometric structures. When used in spells and magic, they offer a great boost to power.

If you would like to use crystals in your magic, reading more about them, knowing how to use them, and being aware of their properties are recommended. However, if you find a crystal that calls to you, placing it on your altar is definitely a good idea, and your intuition can guide you.

Staff

Staffs have been used for centuries in magic. They've been used by druids, shamans, witch doctors, and Wiccans. Staffs are powerful for channeling energy.

Staff can be a simple walking stick charged with energy. It can be carved or decorated with feathers and crystals. They can be simple or elaborate. They have powerful connections to the earth and are great in a group or outdoor magic.

Many Wiccans like to use staffs to enhance their ability to raise and channel energy.

Sword

Many Wiccans enjoy using ritual swords as a tool to channel energy. They, too, are powerful for raising, directing, and focusing energy.

If you elect to use a sword in magic and if the blade is kept sharp, remember to exercise caution, especially if you are working in a group or with someone else.

As you study Wicca and begin to refine your knowledge and practices, you will begin to find tools that work best for you. Your altar will become a representation of yourself and your magical preferences.

You can always experiment and try different tools until you find the one that best resonates with you. This is your starting guide for finding your way on the Wiccan path.

Overview

Thank you kindly for reading through the book *Wicca for Beginners*. Hopefully, you have learned a lot of new information about Wicca and how to follow the Wiccan Path.

Now that you have made it through the Beginner's Guide for Wicca, you should have a basic knowledge of how to practice Wicca, as well as some tools to get yourself started with the practice. If you have any questions or would like to further your studies, there are plenty of additional materials to read and explore.

The first step to take now is to decide whether you want to be in a Coven or practice on your own. Either way, you should also consider getting yourself an altar setup and a Book of Shadows.

Remember that there is no right or wrong way to immerse yourself in the Wiccan lifestyle. Choose what resonates with you and what speaks to you. You are a powerful and incredible life force that has the ability to harness natural magic. Change the world; change your world!

Most of the spells in this book are unique and should provide you with plenty of material to get started with. Magic is at your fingertips! Try the spells you like, or adapt them for different uses! Take a stab at writing your own spells to enhance your personal power.

Finally, if you enjoyed this book and learned some great new information, a review on Amazon would always be appreciated! Thank you again for choosing this book, and Blessed Be.

CPSIA information can be obtained
at www.ICGtesting.com
Printed in the USA
LVHW062031240121
677375LV00008B/264